Charlie,

   I was thrilled to be your godfather when you were such a very special baby.

   Now I am thrilled to be your godfather when you are such a very special man.

                 Uncle Tay

BROOKLYN ODYSSEY

BROOKLYN ODYSSEY

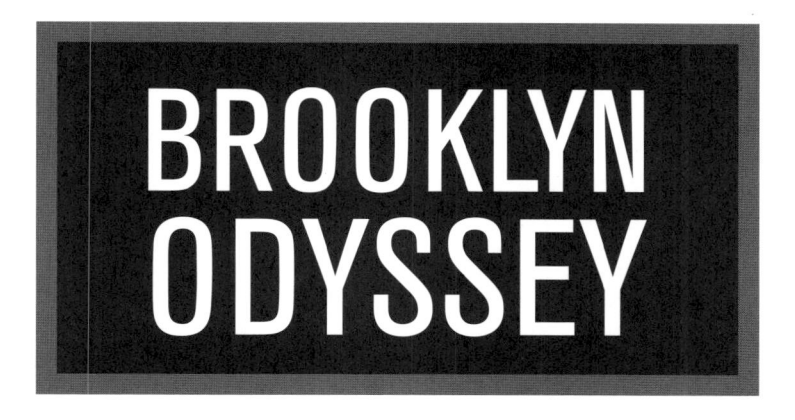

THE ART OF MEN ACTING

BOOK I

❋

Tony Giordano

ANANKE, LTD. New York

Copyright © 2013 by Tony Giordano

All rights reserved. No part of this book may be reproduced in any form without written permission from the publisher.

Cover by: Nicholas Nappi
Editor: Leah Sims

First edition: 2013

Hardcover ISBN: 978-0-9894827-1-4
eBook ISBN: 978-0-9894827-0-7

Printed in the United States of America.

Ananke, Ltd.
% Giordano
13 Circuit Road
Bellport, N.Y. 11713
1 631 803 6013
1 212 947 0443
1 917 592 7212
www.tonygiordano.us
www.brooklynOdyssey.com
tonygiord@aol.com

FOR EVELYN AND VINCENT
Could I have had better parents? Yes. They could have been rich, sophisticated and connected. Then I would be an even bigger brat.

&

FOR ANNA
A better godmother than my Aunt Anna has yet to be born.

&

FOR THERESA
My sister prepared me for a life of love/hate relationships.

ACKNOWLEDGMENTS

THOSE WHO ENCOURAGE YOU TO WRITE BECAUSE THEY ENJOY THE STORIES: JoAnn Tedesco, Michael Mullaney, Ulu Grosbard, Michael Patella, Susan Johann, Jeffrey Hyatt, Joan Valentina, Joan Micklin Silver, Nanjun Li, Theresa Fischer, Joe Sicari, Joe Hindy, Michael Fischetti, Tuck Milligan, Fyvush Finkel.

THOSE WHO ATTEND THE BOOK'S BAPTISM, CONFIRMATION, AND WEDDING: Armand Assante, Mary Joan Negro, Nicholas Nappi.

THOSE WHO READ ONLY THE FINAL DRAFT WITH OBJECTIVITY THAT IS PRICELESS: Karen Whiting, Mark Leib, Guy Gallo, Henry Herx, Peter Morrison.

THE ONE WHO PRODUCES A PUBLIC READING TO LIGHT THE FIRE IN MY BELLY: JoAnn Robertozzi.

HE who provides the Grace.

PREFACE

Family, friends and strangers share our life in "the art of men acting."

BOOK I **BROOKLYN ODYSSEY**
This book encourages everyone to be a brat to attain the best that life can offer. Better able we will then be to share humanity. My journey toward self-actualization occurred when I was very young. Despite humble origins, lack of sophistication, no wealth, no power, and no connections, I was able to find my bliss. Aunt Gracie told me, "Every generation after yours is unaware of how innocent America was, not too long ago, and you should tell them. It may not be too late." So I offer my story as a map for each reader to fulfill his or her personal story.

BOOK II **TONIGHT I WON'T BE ACTING**
After a wonderful life as a freelance theatre director where, thanks to so many productions across America, I had the opportunity to know my country, our society and our corruptions I wrote these anecdotes to view how the good, the bad, the beautiful, and the ugly reveal that while I was enjoying my life as a director our society lost its greatness. And both theatre and I became powerless to prevent the loss.

BOOK III **NOT FOR PROPHET**
This book is written from obscene necessity to expose our faults that are leading us to our demise. My passion was to save the world. But saving the world turned out to be too difficult. For, though birth begins our lives, it is hard to cure the world's woes since we are not present at their creation. Instead we are thrust into life like a suitcase thrown from a fast-moving train. How well we plant our feet on the ground determines how well we can survive. *Not for Prophet* suggests to those who choose to save this world advance warnings they will need.

CHAPTER 1

EARLY MORNING OF JANUARY 26, 1953 a chill hangs over our four-room apartment at 1877 Coney Island Avenue, the same apartment we lived in before we left during WWII. When we returned six years later war had not altered any part of our view, except trolley cars that used to run on tracks changed to buses that now ran under electrical wires. My mother hoped by returning to this apartment we could proceed as if the war had never happened. But life is teaching us that we cannot reenter the womb. The war had happened. We had left. We returned.

Lemon meringue pie sits uneaten and smashed on the porcelain kitchen table, rekindling hot emotions from last night. My mother is dressed for work, rinsing the breakfast dishes. She rails at me.

"After today, no more scenes. Remember, an agreement is an agreement."

As Theresa rushes through the kitchen she responds to my mother.

"You gotta be kidding. He'll never give in."

I'm blocking Theresa's way. She has a way of making demands that accompany a willingness to punch me as often as possible.

"Move!"

I clear a path and notice for once she doesn't push me backwards.

I yell back at my mother, "You too! After today no more scenes!"

I am dressed in my colorful argyle, V-neck sweater. The apartment buzzer ends the squabble. My mother heads out of the kitchen, calling over her shoulder.

"Theresa, tell your father Frank's here."

Theresa taps the bathroom door, "Frank's here."

I grab my zippered beige suede jacket and slip out of the apartment. Mom leans out the window overlooking Coney Island Avenue as Frank returns to his Sanitation Officer's car. Dirty piles of snow border the curbs. She calls.

"Frank?"

And gets his attention.

"Vinnie'll be right down."

"Helen, can we give you a ride?"

"No thanks, Yetta and I are meeting at the bus station. We have the union this morning."

My mother calls to me as I exit the building.

"Anthony, you have money?"

Yesterday I turned fourteen. I shout up to her.

"Aunt Anna gave me five dollars for my birthday."

She shouts back, taking the opportunity to taunt me.

"They're not gonna let you in. Why waste your time?"

For once I am smart enough to hold my tongue as she stares at me with the pain usually reserved for mothers watching sons go off to war. When I refuse to respond, she closes the window. I stand at a distance and watch Theresa exit the building. She is four years older than me, nearly eighteen, athletic, and gorgeous. Her wavy brown hair blows against the wind. She walks with the gait of an athlete, due to her tremendous gifts on a horse, swimming, roller-skating and almost all competitive sports. Theresa is on the Prospect Heights varsity basketball team. She crosses the street, carrying books and a gym bag with sneakers dangling from it. Then my father exits wearing a sanitation officer's uniform and hat, stares after me, curious as to whether his son will be a boy or a man by nighttime, but says nothing. He goes to the passenger side of the car, and Frank pulls away. Last, but never least, my mother comes to the street, places garbage in the pail, her face ablaze in eternal wisdom of mothers who know life is often not a blessing.

✳

WE LIVED IN THIS APARTMENT the first time until 1944. I had been born nearly six years earlier, the year *Gone With The Wind* was produced, television was being manufactured, *Superman* was created, The *Wizard of Oz* opened, and Hitler was instigating World War II. World dynamics were so hot my birth did not receive attention. But I was well born by nature nevertheless, named Anthony ("God given") then baptized Eugene ("well born"), a kind of aristocrat in any surroundings, possessing two great gifts: curiosity and courage. Personally speaking, *Superman, Gone With The Wind, Hitler, The Wizard Of Oz,* television, and World War II did not receive any attention from me either. During the first six years of my life. I had an indefatigable ability to keep my family on their toes by bugging them with questions they could never answer, all the topics they avoided.

"Who am I?"

Silence. No answer from anyone.

"How did I get here?"

"What do you mean?"

"Where did I come from?"

"Ask your mother."

"Mom, how did I get here?"

"Ask your father."

"He told me to ask you."

"God sent you."

"How?"

"You just appeared one day."

"Really?"

"Yes."

"Where was I before?"

"Enough with the stupid questions. Stay out of here. I have to wash the kitchen floor."

"Theresa, guess what!"

"What?"

"I didn't come from anywhere. I just appeared one day."

"Good. Someday you will disappear."

"I think I came from Heaven."

"You're a jerk. Did you know that? A real jerk."

Fortunately I was clever enough to realize that the world surrounding me was not put together with spit and spittle. And though I had an instinct that the world was in trouble I had no desire to disappear. Instead I began to search for an alternate world, the one from which I could get answers so I could save the world. Most idealistic children dream in this fashion until they reach the age of reason. In my case reason never smothered that dream.

My father, Vincent, was the fourth of eleven children born to Italian American parents. He dreamed of becoming a pharmacist until he was asked to leave high school and provide for his younger brothers and sisters. He managed to perform this service with such abandon that from that time onward he lived totally in the present, accessible to each moment and to everyone. Due to the warmth of his character, the all-American nature of his personality, and the innate sense of leadership within him, my father became the paternal figure throughout the family. To me he looked like a cross between Dana Andrews and Clark Gable. Years later when I directed Dana Andrews, I knew I was right.

My mother, Evelyn (called Helen by her family for no other reason than "They felt like it"), was the third oldest child in her family, and like my father was born to Italian American parents. They had sixteen pregnancies, and though only eleven of them were born, the family was more often than not behind the economic eight ball. My mother, like my father, abandoned her dream by the time she was twelve, that of becoming Myrna Loy. So painful must have been this loss that at fourteen when she became a seamstress in a factory, she dedicated the remainder of her life to believing that dreams hurt and are therefore bad. In her commitment to marriage and family, she was par excellence. She and my father created the perfect marriage. Family and home were goals they embraced with loving obsession. This gave me too much comfort at home so I longed for excitement from the world.

Until Theresa was three-and-a-half years old, she was the princess and the apple of our father's eye. But the day I was brought home from the hospital Theresa's world exploded and, consciously or unconsciously, she set out to destroy mine. I guess conflict must come from somewhere. If your parents refuse to be your enemy, your sister must take on the role, and she did. I wooed Theresa, but she withheld affection. I was so sensitive to her rejections that Theresa was able with ease to turn my parents' prince into her personal toad in a flash.

Unlike me, Theresa was a chip off the old block. She was trying to play by the rules of our family rather than inventing her own. She fit into the family's humble origins. I did not. My life was precious and I knew it. Theresa asked for permission to do things. I never did. For me asking was a waste of time in a family where "no" was the immediate response to any request. Theresa never realized that you had to break the rules, move forward, and prove how ably you could do what they would have said no to, at which point they would smile in admiration.

We were an average family of four: father, mother, sister and brother.

※

OUR SECTION OF BROOKLYN IS FLATBUSH, where by noontime on Sundays, following church, dinner is served. Even when we lived here the first time people return to their apartments with bagels, newspapers, and general supplies to end the week. From a third-story, modest four-room apartment, my mother creates a comfortable castle, filled with aromas of great food. Theresa and I share a bedroom. Theresa is nearing nine years old and isn't thrilled we sleep in the same room. My parents have their bedroom. We also have a living room, where Theresa sleeps most nights, and a kitchen with a porcelain table for four. What is astonishing is how my mother manages on holidays to invite all the relatives. She and my father set up tables everywhere and my mother cooks soup to nuts for thirty people. You would have to have met my mother to witness her skill at this. Her spotless housekeeping and her culinary talents are matchless, except for her sisters, my aunts, who share similar skills. During the weekend Mom prepares delicious foods for the rest of the week when she returns from work and completes her consistently great meals. Mom is a sergeant at arms. Though Sundays are Mom's specialty, never a night during the week passes without a substantial dinner.

Peace exists on this lovely summer day in 1944 as if danger could never reach our uneventful neighborhood though the war is winding up its swing to punch us in the face. The air is filled with Judy Garland's "Somewhere Over the Rainbow" coming from a radio in a neighboring apartment just at the moment my mother's dinner is ready. I am an average six-year old boy, free to roam into trouble with the five-year old Lillian.

While stirring macaroni in a pot of boiling water, Mom orders Theresa, who is twisting the string on a stuffed bracciole.

"Find him."

Instead of obeying, Theresa wraps the cord around the meat as if she is wringing my neck.

"Go, or he won't eat today."

"He never listens to me."

Aggravated, my mother puts her wooden spoon on the stove and crosses through the apartment to a bedroom window overlooking Coney Island Avenue.

"Anthony! Anthony!! Anthony!!!!!!!"

She returns when it is obvious I am nowhere in earshot.

"Get your brother."

"He won't eat anyway. Thinks he's Fred Astaire . . ."

My mother grabs the string.

"Stop! What are you doing with this?"

Theresa finishes her sarcasm, ". . . dancing in the movies. What a jerk!"

"Don't be such a pain in the ass, Theresa. For once let's enjoy a Sunday dinner."

Theresa storms out of the apartment, past my father, who is reading the Sunday papers in the living room. He abandons the papers and as my mother drains the macaroni into her colander, comes into the kitchen wearing a baseball coach's uniform.

"The game starts in an hour. He's not interested."

"He'll go with you," she declares, pouring sauce.

My father eyes her, turned on. She knowingly asks, "Whatta you looking at?"

She brings the bowl of macaroni to the table. They laugh together, sexy, as my father sits to eat. They are a couple. My sister and I are not. On the avenue Theresa shouts over a passing trolley.

"Anthony!!!! Anthony!!!!!!!!!!"

Then she calls to the owner who is sweeping in front of his candy store.

"Fyvush, you see my brother?"

Fyvush indicates the next building.

"With Lillian."

Theresa climbs to the second floor, sees the apartment door ajar, and enters as *"Somewhere Over The Rainbow"* is coming to an end. She calls.

"Anthony!"

Lillian and I, both naked, turn toward the sound as Theresa enters the living room. She's shocked.

"What are you two doing?"

I answer simply.

"Dancing."

Theresa flings my clothes to me.

"You're gonna get killed."

"Why?" I ask in real innocence as I put my shorts and T-shirt on.

"Where's your mother, Lillian?"

"At my uncle's."

Theresa is in her glory, reveling in her chance to torture us.

"Aren't you both ashamed of yourselves?"

"We're dancing," I insist.

Theresa pushes me out of the apartment, then smacks me in the face. I rush ahead carrying my shoes, and up the stairs in our building into the bathroom. Theresa enters the kitchen in her role, now, as mother.

"Your precious son was naked with Lillian in her apartment."

My parents suppress amusement to avoid aggravating Theresa. My mother ventures first.

"Where is he?"

"Hiding."

Theresa sits to eat heartily. Mom calls.

"Anthony, come and eat before it gets cold!"

Theresa thirsts for my blood.

"Aren't you gonna give it to him?"

Mom tells her only in an effort to appease. "Don't worry. He'll get it."

I enter, wiping my washed face. Mom addresses me.

"Come and eat."

"No, thank you. I just had a baked apple."

My parents laugh. My mother is interested.

"Baked apple? What are you talking about?"

Theresa is fit to be tied.

"Fyvush tells him to avoid things he doesn't like with this stupid baked apple thing."

I pick up my cue.

"He says it always gets a laugh. And he was right. You both laughed."

Theresa is filled with belligerence.

"I didn't laugh."

I get my dig in, knowing I am now home and protected by adults.

"You never laugh."

Mom offers, "If you like baked apples, why didn't you tell me? I'll make them."

"He doesn't like baked apples! He's trying to get out of a beating. Can't you ever see what he's doing?"

Though only a scrawny kid, I know how to change a topic.

"Fyvush was in the vaudeville."

My mother is my best sparing partner.

"There's a war on now. Don't let Fyvush fill your head with stupid things. Vaudeville!"

I push my food away, an insult to my mother.

"I'm not hungry."

"If you don't finish that entire plate, you're not going to the ballpark today."

"It's too much food for me."

"You'll sit there all afternoon and eat even when it gets cold."

Theresa hates hypocrisy. "He won't eat and you'll let him go anyway. And you know it."

"Mind your p's and q's. You always have something to say."

Theresa spits out her insult across the table to me.

"Brat."

My father decides to calm us.

"What were you doing at Lillian's?"

My mother blocks his question by pushing the food back to me.

"Eat and go with them."

"I can't eat all that."

My mother caves easily. "Eat half of it then."

Theresa is getting ready to murder us.

"He gets whatever he wants and you tell me to shut up."

Cutting Theresa off, "Fyvush traveled all over the world."

My mother always engages with me.

"Dreaming will get you nowhere. Keep your feet on the ground. War on today you never know what's gonna happen. Europe is going insane."

My father has been waiting.

"I asked you a question."

"What?"

"What were you doing at Lillian's?"

"He was naked! That's what he was doing!"

Theresa is frustrated that she's repeated this again and again without once getting the reaction she's hoped for.

"Why were you naked?"

Mom comes to the rescue once again.

"Eat before it gets cold."

"I'm waiting. How did you get naked?"

"I took my clothes off."

My mother laughs, revealing whose side she's really on.

"Then what happened?"

"We danced."

"Why did you take your clothes off to dance?"

"You know."

My father is serious. "No, I don't know."

My mother brings the topic to an end.

"What difference does it make? They're little kids. What could happen? Let him eat."

Theresa shows fangs. "If I did that, I'd get a beating."

Off the hook, I announce.

"I'm gonna be a dancer."

My mother loves my antics.

"Oh sure, tomorrow. Don't forget. Where do you get these silly ideas?"

"Fyvush says his whole family sang, danced, and played musical instruments."

My mother stores ironies for these occasions.

"Now he owns a candy store, so what good did it do him?"

"He showed me how to do bells."

"Bells? What are bells?" my father wonders.

I rise from the table, jump straight into the air sideways, try to kick both feet to one side, and end up crashing to the floor instead. This gives them a full-bodied laugh, bonding us as a family, at my expense. My father instigates more fun.

"Oh, bells! Now I understand. Want to do it again?"

Without the slightest embarrassment I explain "I have to practice."

My mother teases.

"Is Fyvush gonna pay the hospital bill when you break your neck?"

I ask, sneaking in something thought about but never mentioned.

"Can I take lessons?"

This surprises my father.

"Dancing lessons? Nobody in our family ever goes in for dancing."

"So what? I want to."

He is always the reasonable man.

"Well it's easier to do things your family can help you with."

"I don't like those things."

Theresa grinds her teeth.

(To me) "You turn my stomach."

She storms off to the bathroom.

My father suggests, "Hurry and eat. You can be batboy today."

"I don't want to be batboy."

"You'll get along better in life if you can do things other people do."

"I don't want to do things other people do."

"I can't keep up with you. Last week you were angry because I left without you."

"I wanted to watch, that's all."

Mom is caving.

"Well hurry and eat, and go with them. Figure it out when you get there. Children in China would be happy to have this food, believe me."

I push the plate to her.

"Then mail it to them. I'm not eating it."

She moans.

"People must think I don't feed you. Put some meat on those bones."

My mother's brothers, Uncles Andy and Willie, in baseball uniforms, enter our apartment and then the kitchen, carrying a pan. Andy tells my father,

"Let's go coach, our last game. Next month you, Willie and I will be pitching against Adolf."

Willie hands a pan to Mom.

"Anna made you eggplant parmigiana."

My dad rises and starts out with Andy and Willie. Theresa returns from the bathroom, wearing a baseball shirt. My mother whispers to me.

"Hurry. They're leaving."

I use my best weapon. "I can't eat it. It tastes funny!"

The proud cook recoils. "Tastes funny? Learn to keep your mouth shut if you know what's good for you."

Through closed teeth "I kknnoow whhat's gooooddd for meeeee!"

Amused, as always, "Mr. Big Shot! Get outta here! You'll eat this later."

I slam the door as I exit to punctuate my victory, but as I run down the stairs my mother opens the door and shouts loud enough to win the last word.

"That mouth is gonna get you into trouble! Mark my words!"

I ate none of her food and went to the game anyway, just the way Theresa had predicted. Mom hated the insult to her cooking but let me step right over her. Not bad for a six-year-old! I had my mother's spunk. In fact, we were very similar. We both had to win, but she willingly lost because she loved the fact that her son could beat her. It was always reputed that she stood behind the slammed door with her signature grin whenever I won. It made her aware that I was capable of stepping through her as if she was the fullback I had to knock down to prove I could handle myself.

Evelyn, Vinnie, Theresa, and Anthony. Four basically different people created our family dynamic. The psychological nature of human beings is that we either clash or relate. In most cases we clash, at least in some way. Theresa could not bear my freedom as her younger brother, because our parents seemed to give me total permission to be myself. And though I feel that is slightly untrue, meaning they never actually gave me such freedom, I will admit that I took my freedom and that they condoned it because I was the boy.

Theresa had real love/hate towards me. Surprisingly she was the most trust worthy person I ever met in life, despite being a force for me to deal with. And though I had trouble understanding how someone could be so trustworthy and so outrageously angry simultaneously, in time when I began to think from her point of view, I realized how difficult it was for Theresa to suffer fools gladly. She saw life in black and white and refused to tolerate anything less than what she assumed to be the right way, which, in my opinion, too often was the old fashioned way.

Theresa had my father's athletic prowess. Virtually from birth she swam, played baseball, and rode horses. At Prospect Heights High School she was on the varsity basketball team. Though she should have, she never pursued sports professionally because she adhered to society's game plan of marriage and family forced upon her as a result of unquestioned Italian American traditions. She never fought to establish her own plan. It is possible it never dawned on her to chuck aside plans that were not of her making.

Theresa was a knockout. Because she was a great athlete and a beautiful girl, she should have had it all, but she never discovered how to use either her athleticism or her beauty. Thus she spent her life in resentment of my freedom. She simply saw in me a brat (all too true) and felt I should obey the world we grew up in, its rules and clichés. She was unwilling to accept my outspoken tongue and thought I should obey my parents even though they never tried to make me obey them. So whenever I refused, she wanted to punch my clock. Theresa played the role of parent. Frustrations with each other left me with no sister. So I fought my battles alone, which is why, eight years later, I travel by myself this morning to pursue my Odyssey.

❋

DURING THE CHILLY SUBWAY RIDE, I struggle mentally to offset the sound of the train's wheels echoing my mother's irritating prediction.

"They're not gonna let you in. Why waste your time?"

With each subway stop across Brooklyn, the fire in my belly flickers as if it might go out and leave me with three strikes against me, for prior to my fourteenth birthday I already lost two important battles, struck out twice trying to find the life I want to live. I had hoped to be a song-and-dance man during the war, but the family made fun of my voice and my movements. A song-and-dance man does not come home for dinner every evening and doesn't return at the end of each week with a paycheck. After the war, I wanted to play classical piano, but they refused to even buy the piano.

But let me confess, I am being disingenuous by making it seem the obstacle to my being a song-and-dance man was my family. The obstacle was my lack of talent. I screeched when I sang from the inability to hold a tune in one key. And my dancing had certain arthritic movements, the natural extension of a skinny kid with scoliosis. And, of course, the work ethic in our family was well established. My grandparents emigrated from Italy as little children and kept their noses to grindstones in gratitude for being in America. My family was now made up of proud descendants who welcomed only honest work with a weekly check, as proof of emancipation from the slavery of having been peasants for centuries. They survived the depression and were not about to take chances. They were content by the time I came into the world, and they wanted for nothing other than what they had. They embraced the basics in life as luxuries: a clean home, a warm bed, terrific food, and family members who live close by. I was the fly in their ointment by dreaming that life could be different, and of course by different I meant better. Can you imagine how frustrating for them to have me as a member of this family, a malcontent who wanted all the things they denied themselves; but also how frustrating for me to have such a content family? It would require exorcism to break from the shackles of their contentment. So this morning it was urgent that I never lose another battle. Or, three strikes I'm out.

❊

AT 8:55 A.M. I ENTER Brooklyn Preparatory School, renowned for its academic traditions and classical education. I am instantly smothered by the thunderous cacophony of preppies wearing blazers and ties, so I am totally out of place in my zipped up suede winter jacket. Pushing my way through the dense crowd, I overhear diverse student conversations. One upperclassman tells fellow seniors.

"The cows eat it, then we drink it. When it assimilates it doesn't become less effective, just absorbed. It's still radioactive."

He and his friends keep moving so I am unable to follow their point. Then a younger student, possibly a junior, seems to be advising freshmen.

"They never teach until you study the material first. Each class starts with a five-minute quiz to be sure you did your homework."

The freshman replies.

"That doesn't make sense."

The junior clears the matter up.

"It's not really stupid. If you studied the material but didn't understand it, you have questions for the teacher right after the quiz."

A debating team member is bragging about last night's debate.

"Once they started on World War II, I knew we were in for the bronze at least. Charlie drilled us all semester. St. John's didn't have a chance. We won everything."

His friend is thrilled and announces to others.

"Brian says we took the gold."

The debater continues.

"By eleven fifteen we had covered every invasion firsthand. No way we couldn't take the gold. I got home at one, studied for the physics test till four, and plan to sleep through the weekend. I drank three cups of coffee to get here on time."

A Jesuit pushes his way through the thick crowd, holding a pack of essays over his head. Brian shouts to him.

"Father, I get a ninety?"

"Your only ninety today, Brian, is your temperature."

A loud bell rings.

In a flash, students rush to classes so quickly it's as if they evaporate. Suddenly the corridor is empty and painfully quiet. I am alone in this spotless hallway. It echoes long traditions that seem like being in what I imagine to be Europe, perhaps, some earlier century, or a monastery on the side of a Tibetan mountainside, anywhere but the center of Brooklyn. It is all so Spartan. There are black wrought iron bars outside the windows, so when the sun reflects against them, they make mosaic patterns on the floors and walls. There are dark polished floors, shiny wooden oak doors, and half-paneled wooden walls below an off-white patina that looks like vanilla ice cream. I know instantly many generations of boys my age have been here. This building is Mediterranean in essence, Spartan in look, warm and comfortable to fit a person my size.

I see the sign: Headmaster.

So I enter.

A pretty secretary, in a small office, glances up from her typing. On her desk is a poinsettia plant.

"Yes?"

"I would like to see the headmaster."

"He's not here."

"Will he be back?"

"Not today."

"Oh."

She senses my stunned reaction.

"I mean he is not scheduled to be in till late."

Slightly relieved, I say, "Oh."

She looks up.

"Can I help you?"

"May I wait?"

"I mean this afternoon."

"What?"

"Father won't be back till this afternoon."

"May I wait?"

She stops typing.

"It's nine a.m."

"Yes, I know."

"He's at a conference in New York. Perhaps I can help."

"No, thank you."

"Could you tell me what you want to see Fr. Watson about?"

"Well, I would rather talk to him."

"Maybe it's something he can't help you with."

"I would still rather talk to him."

"Why don't you come back later?"

"I don't live around here."

"Does he know what you want?"

"No."

"Does he know you're here?"
"No."
"Does he know you?"
"No."
"Perhaps his assistant, Fr. Ryan, could help you?"
"No, thank you."
"You'd have to wait all day."
"I don't mind."
"Wouldn't it be better to tell someone else what you want?"
"I want to see the headmaster."
"He'll be in all day tomorrow."
"Tomorrow will be too late."
"Why don't you sit over there then."
Anxiously, "Will he definitely be back?"
"Definitely."
"I mean today."
"He said he would."
"Thank you."

The secretary gets up and takes letters into the connecting office. I stretch my neck to notice that the headmaster's office has an outside entrance.

I sit.

I wait.

※

I HAD NO APPETITE so every Sunday I find clever ways to avoid eating. Pretty good power I'd say from a scrawny little kid! Like that Sunday I had not eaten one morsel but went to the ballpark anyway. Unfortunately, once there, I was given the job of batboy. My father and my mother's brother Alfred coach this sandlot ball team, which is made up of other uncles, cousins, and neighbors. Everyone has a routine, except me. Theresa goes to the snack truck to help Uncle Tommy sell hot dogs, soda and beer.

I drop two heavy bats as soon as the first batter swings two other bats, ten feet from home plate. I run over to him.

He asks, "What do you want?"

"The bat."

"I'm not finished."

"I'll wait."

My father rushes over.

"Anthony! Anthony."

He walks me to the rack of bats.

"What are you doing?"

"You told me it was my job to get the bat."

"When he's finished with it, I meant. Stay here until he's finished. Do you understand?"

"Yes."

As my father runs back to coach first base, the batter throws one bat and starts walking to home plate. I am about to run to get the discarded bat. My father yells.

"Stop! After he hits the ball. Or three strikes, he's out! Then get both bats at once."

The "three strikes, he's out" irritates the batter.

The game begins. The umpire yells.

"SSSTTRRRIKKKKE 1!"

I look to my father, who shakes his head "no." I look to the batter, who emphatically shakes his head "no" to me, with blood in his eyes.

"STRRIKKEEE 2!"

Again I look to my father, who holds up three fingers. The batter does a furious double take. Then the batter hits a ground ball and as he runs to first base he flings his bat aside without noticing that I'm running toward him. The bat hits me in my thigh with the pain I hope I never feel again. There is a gasp from the bleachers, which stops the game. My father and other players run over to massage me. Theresa laughs loudly and rushes to enjoy my latest tragedy. When I see her, I try to suppress the pain. Somehow Theresa is always present at my humiliations.

My father assures me.

"You'll be all right."

Uncle Alfred tries to be helpful.

"Why don't you rest in my car?"

My father comes to my rescue.

"We'll let him be water boy. Theresa will be batboy."

Theresa gloats while my father leads me to a bucket and a water pipe in the ground.

"When a player wants water hold the bucket out and hand him the spoon. Okay?"

This seems odd to me.

I wonder, "Why can't they get their own?"

The opposing coach yells over to my father.

"We playing?"

"We're ready," my father assures him.

What follows is a nine-inning montage with players drinking water while always looking away toward the game, using the water to rinse their mouths and then spitting it out. I try to avoid their spit by making countermoves that always seem to place me in the wrong position for the ultimate spit until I become what people refer to as a drenched rat. Between saliva, sun, sweat, blisters on my hands, and grime of the field, I cannot help but wonder why my family would, if I give them the chance, choose this as a goal for me. My father is aware that I am least likely to succeed in his world, which I openly disdain anyway.

As I pass my mother in our sunset filled apartment, she laughs with a mouth full of insult as soon as she sees me. I refuse to respond. I go straight into the kitchen. I know what I look like and this enforces her image of me as her awkward-though-amusing son who doesn't eat enough to have the kind of muscle necessary to conquer the world so, in her opinion, I should forgo "Such big ideas." My mother always enjoyed telling me the reason there are no naked pictures of me as a child, a vogue of the time, was because *You had so many broken bones you looked like a plucked chicken.* In a rich family they might have recognized scoliosis and hired some doctor to cure it. But no, I was simply a plucked chicken so no one ever thought of treating the problem. In my family life itself and all the awful things life can do to you has the right to play a starring role, so you should grin and bear a curved spine. My mother has an odd sense of humor, one determined to keep me humble, and she worked at it with impressive skill. Not that there was a lack of love, but clearly my mother assumed the world would eat me up and her negativity would protect me. Besides, Italians are not like Jews.

In a Jewish family there is immediate support: *"My son, the doctor!"* An Italian mother prefers to keep you close to home, crippled if need be: *"Help yourself, the refrigerator is full."*

My father and Theresa enter the apartment. Unlike me, they enjoyed a tremendous day of sunshine, fresh air, and exercise.

My father asks, "What's to eat?"

"Roast beef and salad. If you want leftover macaroni, I'll heat it up."

"A sandwich sounds great."

As they enter the kitchen they see my head on top of the table and assume I'm asleep, but as usual I'm just quietly hiding to hear their conversation. Mom whispers.

"Who won?"

"Seven to two, them," he whispers back.

Theresa yells, "What else is to eat?"

"Sssh, keep your voice down. Let him sleep."

This, of course, is an invitation for Theresa to get louder.

"Who the hell is he anyway?"

She rushes out of the room now that her anger is rekindled. Little by little, Theresa's negativity became one of my blessings, for I learned to simply not notice her, which forced me to trust in my own power to take care of myself. Besides, Theresa was encouraging my question. Her continual *"Who the hell does he think he is?"* became mine.

"Who am I?"

※

AS I SIT QUIETLY in the secretary's office, a priest with a stack of folders enters.

"Is the secretary here?"

"Yes. She's in the headmaster's office."

"Thank you," he responds.

"You're welcome."

He sees the door ajar, speaks to the secretary, "I'm leaving the Greek grades on your desk. Juniors."

"Thank you."

He smiles at me as he exits. The secretary comes back in.

"He's Fr. Culkin. I'm Nancy Doherty."

"Irish?"

"Some English and a bit of German. You?"

"Anthony Giordano."

"Italian, obviously."

"All four grandparents."

"Speak it?"

"No."

"Does anyone in your family speak Italian?"

"No. My mother can understand and speak just a little. But my father doesn't."

"That's too bad. Were they born in Italy?"

"No. They were all born here except my grandparents who came over as little kids and grew up here."

"You have a large family?"

"Yes."

"Are you very close?"

"My relatives do everything together."

"That's nice. I bet they're a lot of fun."

"Yeah, they're great."

Nancy records semester grades.

I watch.

I wait.

※

A BEACH DAY IS PROOF of my family's fun. Six years old at Coney Island I am speaking with my twenty-nine-year-old godmother, Aunt Anna. Forty inches tall with a humpback, she wears a cotton skirt and blouse to the beach rather than a bathing suit. She sits under an umbrella, measuring an unfinished argyle sweater against me. My bathing suit exposes my twisted spine. Together we're perfect models for a Toulouse-Lautrec painting without color, for at this time in America color is non-existent. Clothes have faded patterns from being washed so often. Rarely does any color jump out at you, so the colors Aunt Anna uses to knit my sweater are especially striking. And because her design and color combination is unique this sweater will always celebrate her artistry.

"It itches."

"Just relax. I need to measure it."

"It's too big."

"Well I'm making this sweater so you can have it when you are older. If I knit your size, you'll wear it out in no time. It's a lot of work and you should enjoy it as long as possible."

When Aunt Anna was ten years old, in the early '20s, doctors encased her in a huge cast over her upper body and head, for reasons no one ever understood. During the two years of this enclosure her spine grew, but she didn't, and her spine twisted into a hump. From the age of twelve, she became forever after a short person even after doctors tried machines to stretch her. Such was medical care for poor people in her day.

Aunt Anna's abilities in the kitchen were staggering. She had an inexhaustible energy to see a task to its finish, no matter how many people she was cooking for. Stools and chairs were in her reach at all times, and I watched her on dozens of occasions perch on a chair overlooking a pot of minestrone soup she had nursed from scratch. She was definitely the family centerpiece. It is true that her tragic youth motivated much of our special love for her, but the real reason was Aunt Anna's strength. Everyone depended on her, needed her, and enjoyed talking to her. Having overcome the agony of those primitives who encased her, she faced life so fully almost everyone could find something of one's self somewhere inside the enormous depth to her character.

Aunt Anna had a friend who occasionally visited for tea, a friend who always expected a crystal stem glass of whisky alongside her cup. "Aunt Belle" was probably seventy at the time, and very genteel, Victorian. I would sit on her lap and dip my finger into her whisky, helping her finish it. I loved listening to the respect for age Aunt Anna showed this lady. Our family believed that anyone you invited into your home became family. Throughout my youth, my mother informed me never to ask friends if they wanted something to eat but to put the food on the table in an appealing way, so they would eat it. She felt that people are too shy to say yes if you ask, and you must make them comfortable.

Perhaps because of her suffering, Aunt Anna had the clearest lens in viewing life I have ever witnessed. Her point of view lacked sentimentality and fantasy. She was super-realistic, and out of this spirit flowed a precision of thought on topics and people that could be funny or sad in a flash. Perched on top of the truth, she could communicate her needs instantaneously. We went grocery shopping through Brooklyn like the Toulouse-Lautrec couple we were. She made no excuses for her size and never felt inadequate to any task. You had only to be with her in the butcher shop to know how powerful this little lady could be.

She was possibly the first person I met who talked. And with original ideas! There was wisdom inside Aunt Anna because of her willingness to deal with reality. She never treated me as a child, nor did I ever act like a child when I was with her. We were friends. We spoke openly about life and death, the economic depression, and her spine.

"You're different than everyone else in the family, Anthony. I don't know what you have, but you have it. Don't let anyone take it away from you. And I mean anyone, you hear?"

I nod assent.

"When you lose who you are, you lose everything. Never forget that."

She was the perfect godmother.

Despite this hot beach day, Aunt Anna continues to measure my new sweater against my skinny chest.

Aunt Anna, how do I learn to dance?

"We never did such things. Take dance lessons, I guess. How else do you learn? But your parents are right. With this war on nobody knows what we're doing. War makes everyone crazy, which in our family is easy. We're all crazy to begin with."

I keep complaining.

"It's itchy."

"At the rate you're growing, I'd have to knit every day of my life otherwise."

"If it's too big, how am I gonna wear it?"

"You'll roll up the sleeves and the waist until you grow into it. Twenty years from now, this sweater will still fit you."

Aunt Gracie, twenty-six years old, beatific and fat, grabs two hands full of food and starts to walk away from the blanket area.

Aunt Josie, my twenty-five-year-old tougher aunt, steps in front of Gracie.

"Where you going?"

Gracie gestures toward beach strangers.

"Maybe some of these people are hungry."

Josie will have none of this.

"If they're hungry, they'll buy frankfurters. What are we, charity?"

Everyone laughs.

Josie takes the sandwiches away from Gracie.

Gracie bemoans.

"What if they have no money?"

"They have no money, they don't eat. We have no money either. Nobody's worrying about us."

Gracie starts back to get food anyway.

"Well, we brought too much."

Josie pushes Gracie away from the food.

"What we don't eat, we take home. Get your mind off food today. Our Holy Mother, St. Gracie! God must be laughing his head off."

Gracie tries to fight back.

"Don't be so selfish."

Aunt Josie includes my cousins, Junior and Alfred, in her fun.

"Your fat aunt was gonna sneak off and eat it all herself.'

Gracie declares, "I'm not afraid to eat in front of you."

Josie tortures Gracie. "We can see. You're busting out of your bathing suit."

Gracie lies. "It's three years old."

"You bought it April this year. Who are you trying to fool?"

"It shrunk when I went into the water."

Gracie seeks help from Junior and Alfred.

"Aunt Josie makes up stories. Don't pay any attention to her."

Meanwhile my mother shouts to the ocean.

"Vinnie!!!!!!"

Anna teases her.

"Helen, you expect him to hear you?"

My mother becomes frightened as Theresa dives off my father's shoulders. And from her distance on the sand she yells.

"That undertow is too strong!"

Aunt Anna tells me.

"Anthony, your mother sees the undertow from here!"

My mother insists, "I can feel it."

Anna enjoys the silliness of this and calls to everyone.

"Helen feels the undertow!"

My grandmother, a bountiful Santa Claus type, joins in.

"Helen, Vinnie knows what he's doing. Go swim with them. See for yourself."

"I don't go in the water. You go, Ma."

"Me? Swim? With all those people peeing in the ocean?"

Everyone laughs.

"But you want me to go in?"

"Eh! It doesn't bother everybody, but when I want a bathroom, I go to a bathroom, not the ocean."

Uncle Tommy wakes up.

"Where's the bathroom?"

Aunt Josie answers him with an edge of disdain in her voice.

"Near the boardwalk, where else?"

He walks in that direction.

Gracie sees an opportunity to sneak back to the food by offering it to one of my cousins, a goodwill gesture that fools no one.

"Junior, you want peppers and eggs? Maybe half, we'll share it."

But Josie is always on guard.

"Gracie's at it again! Gracie, you're gonna blow up like a blimp today."

Gracie gobbles half a sandwich in one gulp.

Aunt Rosie, the hard-of-hearing wife of uncle Tommy, shouts.

"I'll take a veal cutlet!"

Then, louder, she shouts toward her husband walking along the hot sand.

"Tommy, you want peppers and eggs?"

Anna tries to tell Rosie, "Tommy can't hear you."

But Rosie is too deaf to hear Anna, so she shouts louder for her husband's attention.

"Tommy, roast beef?"

Anna reminds everyone.

"Rosie's deaf."

Then she tries to reach Rosie.

"Rosie?!"

By now Rosie is shouting so hard she could wake up most of Brooklyn.

"Tommy, PROVOLONE???"

Anna tries harder.

"ROSIE!!"

But unable to hear, Rosie continues.

"Tommy! TOMMY!"

Josie and Gracie join Anna for vocal power.

"ROSIE!!!!!"

Rosie turns to look at them, startled they are shouting at her. Everyone laughs, but Rosie doesn't understand. Anna tries to explain the situation to Rosie.

"Tommy can't hear you. I cooked sausages with rabe on Italian bread. Would you like one?"

Rosie asks in too loud a voice.

"Where are they?"

"In the straw bag."

Anna assumes this will calm Rosie. But as Rosie moves to the food she tries to reach her husband, who by now is no longer even in view.

"Tommy?! . . . Tommy . . . RABE WITH SAUSAGES?!?!"

The family laughs hysterically. Junior and Alfred, Tommy and Rosie's sons, wrestle me into a sandy mess. Gracie gives sandwiches to strangers passing by. Josie curses Gracie to everyone's amusement, calling her *puttana*. Anna walks over to brush sand off me, to measure a sleeve. In good fun she advises me.

"Pay no attention or you'll become just like us. We don't know any better. We grew up during the depression, scared of our own shadows. You'll be the first to get out. You're interested in things we never were."

"Get out?"

"Not be afraid. But we can't help you cause we don't know how."

Theresa and my father race back to dry off. My father places his wet arm around Mom.

"The water is beautiful. Come in."

She proclaims to the world at large, "Those idiots in Europe

BROOKLYN ODYSSEY   25

want to destroy all of this. Two kids, government drafts him anyway. Sonsabitches!"

My mother's fear, panic, and anger lead this day into sunset.

※

MY FATHER WAS DRAFTED despite a government that guaranteed fathers of two or more children would not be drafted. My mother began a deep hatred against the government for failing to keep their promise, and her anger lasted her entire lifetime. So movers stack my mother's last piece of hand-carved furniture in their truck, which I watch from the fire escape window while my mother and Theresa clean the kitchen. I am nervous, frustrated, thoroughly confused, and unable to be silent. My mother's anger is hard for me to understand because she never explains her fears. I simply assume my father is going on a great adventure and he should take me, so I can't put two and two together as to why we are moving and why she is so upset.

I complain.

"Grandma and Grandpa don't have enough room. How can we live there?"

She runs out of patience.

"Get off the floor. It's wet."

"Who's gonna live here?"

No answer.

"I want to know."

"Go in the living room. You're in the way of the mop."

"Where's Germany?"

"Enough already with your stupid questions!"

"What does the war have to do with my not taking dance lessons?"

"I said GET OUT!!"

Then she rants to herself.

"Break up my home and our lives for what?"

"I'm not going with you. I can live in Fyvush's candy store."

"Good. One less mouth to feed."

I cross to the window and stare out to watch the movers load the truck in the snow. She yells.

"You and Fyvush can Charleston to China."

"Well I'm staying."

"Let's go. Grandma's waiting for us."

"I'm not going!"

At this point, my mother runs over, grabs me by the hair, and flings me across the room.

"Get your coat on before I kill you today!"

Theresa rescues me, revealing kinder feelings underneath her usual hatred.

"Today is not the time to be your usual pain in the ass, brother."

Theresa's generosity is equal to her animosity. Very confusing. She gives me my coat. Mom puts on her coat in a daze. She then turns for one last look around her empty home, takes the apartment keys, throws them against a wall, grabs my hand, and storms out of the apartment. Theresa follows. My mother rushes down three flights of stairs, dragging me behind her and yelling.

"Goddamn Nazis! Destroy the world for what?"

CHAPTER 2

MY GRANDPARENTS LIVED over a dry goods store, on the second floor, in a sprawling apartment with two long hallways, three bedrooms, and one bath. I recall throughout my childhood that when anyone in the family was sick, the women took shifts through the night to care for the sick one, even though they then had to go to work early in the morning. This family was born with humanity I have never seen anywhere else. But during the two years we lived with them I wanted more than they could offer. I wanted information about the world, the war, Heaven.

My grandfather almost never spoke a word. The women did that. Grandpa was gentle as a ripe pear and filled with unconditional love. He called me his bunny, and I hung onto him like a demented dog to a fire hydrant. When he was near, I was happy. Unfortunately for Grandpa, after work and after dinner, he needed to go to the corner and smoke a stogie with his cronies, then return and go to bed. But because I was shut in during the day, except for school, going out at night with Grandpa was a treat I craved. But my mother and my aunts would have none of this.

As soon as Grandpa would head to the closet, I'd move into battle mode.

"Every night, Anthony, it's the same thing, you get your mother crazy."

"I'm going with you."

I squash my skinny body between Grandpa and the door, blocking his exit so he will have to take me. Grandpa begs.

"Anthony! Your mother said you have to stay home."

Aunt Josie enters the battlefield and grabs my arm.

"Come in and listen to Fibber Magee."

"I'm going with Grandpa."

To make peace, Grandpa begins to take his coat off.

"I'll stay home. It's okay. It's okay."

Then Dottie, my youngest aunt, arrives and knocks my hand off the knob.

"Go, Pa, take your walk."

When she tries to open the door, I break from her hold and grab Grandpa's leg.

Aunt Gracie empathizes with me.

"Take him with you, Pa, for God's sake!"

But my mother arrives to officially declare war.

"Let go of Grandpa. Come on!"

"Why can't I ever go out?"

My mother never worries about how to win an argument. She just makes up whatever is necessary.

"It's after dark. The police don't allow children out."

Then she requests all their hands together.

"Give me a hand with him."

They surround me like a huge octopus. But they're no match for me. I kick. I bite. I scream.

Aunt Gracie gets upset, "Let him go with Pa."

She skips to the closet. "All this fuss. I'll get his jacket."

Aunt Josie threatens her.

"Gracie, mind your business! Go, Pa, go! We'll hold him."

Out of pure rage, I break free from his leg, grab the doorknob, and prevent Grandpa from going out. Skinny, but strong! Rarely was Italian spoken in this family, but at moments like this Grandpa would resort to it.

"Bulla manouna! I won't go. I won't go."

Josie struggles to release my hold on the knob.

"I got his hand. Jesus, you're strong for a little weakling. Let go."

But Dottie has a new game plan.

"I know how to get him."

She tickles me and the instant I release my hand yells, "Now, Pa, hurry!"

I giggle and fall to the floor. My mother and Dottie push Grandpa through the door, lock it to the highest chain out of my reach, then go to the parlor with Josie and Anna. Aunt Gracie tries to ease my suffering.

"Grandpa just talks to his cronies. They smoke those terrible cigars. Then he comes right back, that's all."

I hear the radio being turned on in the parlor.

"Come on, let's listen to *Fibber McGee and Molly.*"

But I sit in my rage like an Indian chief.

"You want to sit here all alone?"

She waits for my answer. But I know better.

"Okay, come inside when you're ready."

Gracie joins the others in the parlor nightly to listen to Fibber McGee, the *Lone Ranger, My Friend Irma, Mr. Anthony,* Jack Benny, Bob Hope, and the *Inner Sanctum Mysteries,* as well as world news. On nights when the news of the war is bad, the women take to various bedrooms to weep. Years later I would recognize much of this in the Irish plays of O'Casey. I loved these women. They were living with fears of the world, so they created a fort at home to protect themselves. Within that fort they had a great time. My nightly battle was basically fun to them. I really wanted to get out, but they assumed I was just being "ornery." And I was too young to be intelligent enough to realize that I was subconsciously fighting to get out because my plan to save the world required that I go out into the world. This war was brought into our home, and it was hurting them.

Other times I wanted to make them happy by singing songs.

"Somewhere over the rainbow, way up high . . ."

"Anthony, shut up, you're giving us headaches."

I guess a voice that screeched wasn't a very pleasant way to relieve their stress. And the high pitch of my childhood voice must have been truly irritating. I did not want to be in their world. And clearly they did not want to be in mine. They were content.

Theresa is usually lurking around me at these times to eat the kill, and this night, sure enough, she watches me as I sit against the apartment door. Always happy about my defeats, she whispers in a tone that signals danger.

"Come here."

I don't respond.

"Did you hear me?"

I don't respond.

"I want to show you something."

"No."

She grabs me by the neck and through teeth clenched to accentuate her power, opens her voice to full force.

"I said come here."

Then she pushes me into our grandparents' bedroom, climbs to the top of their closet, and hands me a wrapped Christmas present.

"These are our presents from Santa Claus."

"Santa's been here?"

"How many times I gotta tell you there's no Santa Claus? This one is yours from Grandma and Grandpa. These are from Aunt Josie. This, Aunt Anna. On Christmas morning they'll tell you Santa Claus came by in the middle of the night and left them. Then you'll know what I keep trying to tell you, there is no Santa Claus."

"If there's no Santa Claus, why does everybody say there is?"

"Because they like to lie to kids. Open it. Don't rip the paper."

I open it. It's pajamas.

"I'll rewrap it. On Christmas morning when they tell you Santa Claus brought you these pajamas, you'll know there's no Santa Claus."

Theresa starts to rewrap. I'm stunned. She's made her point.

"Now get out of here."

I stare at her as I leave, not knowing what to say. She's proving that Santa Claus is a lie. I've always felt bad that Theresa needed to force this truth upon me, because her truths, though they were meant to lead me into the adult world, were always sad.

For all my mother's wisdom, she made an error when she gave Theresa permission to be my guard. "Keep an eye on your brother. Walk him to school and back."

My mother did this over a silly incident when I was in the first grade and came home from St. Edmund's Elementary School and she wondered, "What's that white thing you're wearing around your body?"

She was referring to white official-looking straps over my shoulder, across my chest and surrounding my waist.

"I'm the lieutenant."

"Of what?"

"The hallways."

"Who made you that?"

"The principal. Sr. Hogan."

"And what do you do as lieutenant?"

"I report anyone speaking in the hallway."

"To whom?"

"Sr. Mary Hogan."

"Have you taken names already?"

"Yes."

"Where are they?"

I show her the small pad from my pocket.

"These are friends of yours?"

"Some of them."

"Are you nuts? You can't give the names of your friends to the principal and get them in trouble."

"It's my job."

"Tell Sr. Mary to do the job herself. Take that silly thing off and never wear it again. As for those names, give me that book."

She rips it into small pieces.

"Learn some common sense. What am I raising here? Snitching on your friends."

So my mother told Theresa, "You're responsible for him."

This gave Theresa license to be my jailer. Going to school to read, write, spell, add, and subtract thrilled me beyond description. But assigning Theresa to be my guard gave Theresa her new mantra, "Wipe that smile off your face, or I'll wipe it off for you."

For instance, when I fell in love with Patty Richards, I wrote love letters. They were complete expressions of my devotion to her, offerings to spend the rest of my days with her. I have no idea how I came up with such romance in the second grade, but, in any case, Theresa discovered them and revealed them to everyone. I was mocked for being too young to have such feelings and informed that school was for learning, so I was told to give up my girlfriend. Of course, I paid no attention to their insults. But Theresa tried to put an end to my affections by patrolling my activities with razor blade precision. Everywhere I went in school, I saw Theresa. With the excuse that it was her job, she intruded upon every move I made toward Patty. One afternoon as we were leaving school, I began to chase Patty. Patty ran across the street. A car skidded, spinning around 180 degrees, missing Patty by a quarter of an inch. Patty fell apart, became hysterical, and lo and behold, there was Theresa with her hands around my neck, prepared to mete out punishment for the crime I committed. Patty, meanwhile, was collected by her older sister and rushed home with orders to avoid me at all costs.

Theresa knew that she would be chastised if she told Mom, so she threatened to go to the principal instead, and since I loved school, this became a real threat. I was frightened and faked sickness for three days, overwhelmed by all the pressure. I hid under the blankets moaning about headaches and stomach cramps until Theresa finally took it on the chin and told Mom the truth. I was ordered to mind my p's and q's, and to keep in mind that a little girl almost died for no reason. But if I kept to my studies all would be well again. So I returned to school with my tail between my legs.

As soon as I leave Theresa to her Christmas wrapping and return to the hallway Grandpa returns from his stogie. He puts his hand behind my head and calls me with affection.

"Little bunny!"

He walks me to hang up his coat and hat in the hall closet, then guides me into the dark kitchen. Grandpa turns on the lamp on a side counter, so the kitchen has a warm glow. He goes into the pantry and gets a large yellow onion, takes a sharp carving knife from a drawer, opens the bread box and takes out half a loaf of Italian bread and lays it, along with the onion and the knife, on the clean white porcelain table. I sit at one end, knowing our ritual. Grandpa goes to the Frigidaire and takes out a chunk of Roquefort cheese. On his way back to the table he gathers two small glasses and a bottle of homemade red wine.

Grandpa peels the onion and cuts it in half, throwing the skin away. He hands me the smaller half of the large onion and keeps the larger half for himself. He pulls the bread apart, gives me a chunk, and keeps the heel for himself. He cuts the Roquefort, places a piece in front of me, and keeps a larger piece for himself. He opens the wine, pours a small amount for me, and pours a glass for himself. Throughout this scene, there is silence between us. We eat pieces of Roquefort, chunks of bread, bite our onions, and sip wine. Roquefort, bread, onion, wine.

Roquefort, bread, onion, wine until we finish, smiling at each other all the time. Then Grandpa gathers the knife, glasses, and wine. I return the bread and cheese to their places. Grandpa washes the knife and glasses, and cleans the kitchen table with a washcloth. He turns out the light. Together we walk to the parlor to the sounds of radio voices and our family's laughter. All is well again.

As we enter the parlor Jack Benny is on.

"Oh Rochester! Rochester!!"

"Yes boss?"

"Rochester, I'm thinking of throwing a bachelor party for my brother."

"Your brother is not getting married."

"I know!! That's why it's a bachelor party."

The family laughs.

I ask, "Where do the voices come from?"

Aunt Josie answers. "There are actors in the radio. But if you try to see them, they hide. So don't look."

I raise my eyebrows over Aunt Josie's foolish attempt to get away with telling a kid a stupid thing. I scan the faces of the family to discover shit-eating expressions as if they believe little actors live in our floor-model radio. I wonder about their sanity and, though I didn't know such a phrase at the time, I also wonder about my gene bank.

Such was life in Grandma and Grandpa's apartment, safe and sound, clean, with ample food, even love and fun. But there were no books, no intellectual discussions, no sense of connection to the world, though there were plenty of reasons for them to need answers. The panic inside their chests alone, every second during the war, should have sufficed. The war frightened them, but they made no attempt to understand it. It was just some huge zombie roaming outside our apartment to scare them. So they stayed indoors whenever possible. All the men except Grandpa were in the war. The women kept as much a stiff upper lip as they could, except of course for the crying I would hear inside bedrooms whenever one or more of them heard bad news. It was news they never shared with me and possibly never talked about with each other. The war to this family instigated silent suffering. My mother's mantra remained throughout her life.

"Sonsabitches, two children, they draft him anyway."

She developed rage against war. My mother believed in justice above all, except whenever she lied to win an argument against me. But in these cases, she couldn't keep a straight face and her smile would defeat her lie. I inherited her rage against injustice. So did Theresa. The draft remained my mother's single hate until she died. Then, years after her death, when my father was beginning to fail, he revealed the following to me.

"Come with me for a walk, I need to tell you something."

This was interesting because we were not a family of meetings or formality of any kind. If one of us wanted to speak, we just did. But this moment was clearly different, so we took a walk and sat on a park bench.

"Remember in World War II when Uncle Alfred and I went into the war even though he had three children and your mother and I had the two of you?"

"Yeah."

"The government promised not to draft us because we had children."

"Momma made that very clear throughout her life."

"Well, one Sunday night your uncle and I were taking one of our walks. We were always very close friends. We discovered that we were each depressed that our brothers, brothers-in-law, cousins, and other friends were defending America but we weren't. This felt wrong to us. So we went to a recruiting office and registered, asking them to send us the papers as if we were drafted, and that's how we went to war."

From the bottom of my toes I started an enormous laugh.

"You're telling me this now because you think Momma cannot hear you. But she is listening. You are only moments away from meeting with her. Wait until you walk into Heaven and she gets her hands around your neck to strangle you."

My father joined me in a laugh from his belly as well. He knew there was no way out of confronting her on this issue because he had just spilled the beans. I can only say I am sorry to this day that I wasn't in heaven when they reunited. I guarantee, despite years of anger, she would have admired his choice. My mother loved honor. What a great hero my father was for making such a generous choice. Knowing how important it was for him to be able to live within himself my father refused his legitimate excuse to stay out of war so he could be the man he needed to be for the rest of his life. This was the finest lesson I ever learned from anyone.

❉

DURING THE WAR my only memory of my father occurred from his three-day furlough. Everyone in the family went into preparation to welcome him. Usually my mother, Theresa, and I slept in the same room. This night Aunt Josie was making the double bed and airing the room. Theresa gathered a pillow from her small bed. I was working on my spelling homework. Frank Sinatra was singing "Five Minutes More" on the radio.

Aunt Josie opens the window to let in fresh air while she makes the bed with fresh linens and explains that sleeping arrangements must change.

"For a couple of days, that's all."

Theresa whines.

"There's no place for me to sleep in there."

"You'll sleep with Aunt Dottie. Anthony with Aunt Anna. It'll be a pajama party."

Theresa leaves, disgruntled.

Josie closes the window.

"Aunt Josie . . . spell cousin."

"C-O-U-S-I-N."

"Often."

"O-R-P-H-A-N."

"What?"

"O-R-P-H-A-N."

"No, it's not. Often."

"Orphan. O-R-P-H-A-N."

I cannot understand why she's spelling orphan.

"That's not how you spell often."

She tries another way.

"O-R-P-H-I-N?"

Now I'm openly laughing at her. I spell it.

"Often. O-F-T-E-N."

"Oh, orften! I thought you were talking about a child with no parents."

There is a commotion by our door and different voices.

"They're here!"

So I run to see my mother in a spring coat entering with my father in his army uniform, a vision I will never forget of a man proud of himself and a mother in love. There are many hugs from Theresa, my aunts, Grandpa and Grandma, and me. Grandma tells my father.

"You look wonderful, Vinnie. Those care packages we send come in handy, don't they?"

"You bet. Who made the eggplant?"

Aunt Anna asks, "Did you like it?"

"I loved it."

"I made it. If you didn't like it I was going to tell you Rosie made it."

The family loves this self-effacing kind of humor.

Grandma announces, "We'll eat in half an hour."

My father grabs his duffle bag.

"Anthony, come with me. I have some things for you."

I grab his heavy suitcase and struggle down the hallway. In the background there is so much joy and cooperation. I can hear Aunt Dottie.

"I'll help get dinner ready."

But Grandma responds.

"I'm doing that, you go inside."

"Okay Ma, then I'll set the table. How many are we?"

My mother calls, "Ten."

Aunt Josie is always ready to do something.

"I'll get the glasses."

Where there is food there is always Aunt Gracie.

"I'll bring in the hors d'oeuvres while they're hot."

Aunt Josie yells.

"Gracie, don't eat them all!"

In the bedroom, my father puts his suitcase on top of the bed and opens it.

"These are for you."

BROOKLYN ODYSSEY

The suitcase is filled with a stinking smell. Inside are medals, a German pistol and helmet, a Japanese officer's jacket, a large Nazi flag with the swastika, and a bayonet and a luger pistol. Finally, war enters my life. Europe smells real. Now I understand what all the fuss is about.

"Be careful with the bayonet. It's very sharp."

"Smells funny."

I hold my nose. Actually, it is one of the worst smells I've smelled to this day, except for skunk.

"That's from ammunition and . . . everything."

"How did you get all this?"

"When the enemy is killed, soldiers take souvenirs. I exchanged a German medal for the Japanese jacket on the boat. I figured you've never seen such things and you can play with them."

I begin to touch the jacket as my father turns to leave the room, "Have fun."

From the parlor I hear Aunt Dottie.

"Momma made all your favorites."

My mother adds, "Anna made the lasagna the way you like it."

"I didn't eat on the boat today. I was too excited."

Aunt Gracie tells him, "Willie wrote and said you were together in Paris?"

"We spent three days. He looks great."

My mother jokes. "Did you go to Pigalle? If I know the two of you bums . . ."

"Ah, Pigalle!"

"You did, didn't you? You skunks. Is that what you do with the chocolates we send you?"

Over his shoulder she sees me running towards her down the long hallway and she screams.

"What the hell is that?!"

I'm dressed in the Japanese officer's jacket, the German helmet, with the Nazi flag wrapped and flowing from my shoulders, holding the bayonet ahead of me. I am War Personified, yelling,

"CHARGE!!!! CHARGE!!!!!!!!!!!!"

My mother is apoplectic.

"Ohmygod! What a stupid . . ."

Turning to my father, she demands, "How could you do such a thing?"

My father clearly sees no error in any of this as she drags me to the bathroom.

"These are souvenirs. I want him to have them."

She runs hot water into the bathtub and becomes hysterical.

"I can't believe you would do . . . Souvenirs? I'll never get this smell of death out of this house. I tried everything I could to keep war away from here."

She rips my clothes off and flings me, along with all the booty, into the tub. Theresa witnesses my latest humiliation with her usual grin of satisfaction.

"Ouch! It's hot."
My mother goes into rage.

"Stupid war! Bring all this evil into our home."

I try to stand up for my rights to her deaf ears.

"I was playing."

"Goddamn Germans! Who needs all this? Stinking smell of death!"

She scrubs me with frenzy.

Well, I guess dinner was good. It always was in our family, regardless of troubles, but I do not recall the meal. I also guess my mother and father made up when they slept together, but those are only suspicions now in retrospect.

The next morning I enter the kitchen in pajamas as Grandma is frying meatballs.

"Anthony, guess what's ready."

"That's what woke me up. I smelled them."

"Get your cup."

As I take a mug and fill it with coffee, the first thing I notice outside our kitchen window where we climb onto a rooftop, the poor man's patio, is the Nazi flag drying on a clothesline next to the Japanese officer's jacket and the German helmet. Then I sit at the porcelain table, add milk and sugar to the mug of coffee. Grandma gives me a bowl of fried meatballs. She watches as I drop the first meatball into my coffee, break it apart with my spoon, and eat it, breakfast fit for an Italian grandson.

"God bless you Anthony, what a stomach you have!"

"Grandma, how come you don't go to church?"

"Don't go to church? What are you talking about? Were you up at five thirty this morning?"

"No."

"Well I went to six o'clock mass before anybody else was awake. So don't say I don't go to church."

Laughing, "I don't think so."

"You calling your grandmother a liar?"

"Yes."

Grandma has the best laugh in the world, from her belly like Santa Claus.

"Well, I don't have to go to church to talk to God. I talk to Him while I'm cooking. Besides, who wants to give my hard earned money to that scrawny little Irish priest? He puts it into his purse and buys whisky. His little rummy nose is all red from drinking. I don't work all week for him. God understands."

Teasing her, "I'm going to tell the priest."

"What's he going to do? I'd throw him over my shoulder with one arm. The bishop would find him tied up in a corner."

My grandmother and I are laughing as the family returns from church. My table area is a total mess. I've eaten at least three meatballs so far. Aunt Dottie complains to my mother as they enter the kitchen.

"Where did you get this kid? He doesn't belong to us."

Then she looks at me.

"How can you eat that? You're disgusting."

"You want some, Aunt Dottie?"

She feigns vomiting.

". . . meatballs, milk, coffee, and sugar?"

Grandma defends me.

"Leave him alone. It makes him happy."

"There's one left, Aunt Dottie. I saved it for you."

"Get out of here, you nut, who else would eat that?"

My mother intrudes.

"Get dressed. We're leaving to visit Daddy's family."

"I'm staying and playing with my souvenirs."

I am really angry at her for that hot bath and I want her to know it.

"You're gonna get it today," she threatens.

Aunt Anna is a giant of a human being who always comes to my rescue.

"Helen, let me talk to him. You go get ready."

Grandma warns my mother.

"Helen, you better take those things off the line. The neighbors will be hysterical."

"Oh my God, what was I thinking?"

My mother climbs out the window onto the rooftop. This was not an insignificant issue considering the fact that we lived in a Jewish neighborhood, where my mother was drying a huge Nazi flag with its swastika. The Japanese jacket was the icing on the cake and the German helmet the cherry. I felt vindicated. In my mother's insane frenzy and attack against me (Italian boys know how to torture their mothers), she got caught inside her anger because it was nighttime when she hung these things out to dry.

"Why don't you want to go to visit your father's family?" Aunt Anna wants to know.

"I just don't."

"Your father came all the way from Europe."

"Why do we have to go there?"

"That's your father's family, your family. I thought you liked them?"

"I like them, but they make me feel bad."

"How?"

I have no answer.

"Look, Anthony, you can't fight every battle that comes your way. Otherwise nothing is special. Save your energy for a worthwhile fight. Understand?"

I nod yes.

"Wear your argyle sweater. I want to see how it fits. Okay?"

"Okay."

I watch my mother climb back into the kitchen with my booty and walk away towards the rest of the apartment. Then Aunt Anna takes her church hat off, climbs a chair, and puts spaghetti into a pot of boiling water. Every time she performed any of her chores, with this kind of ingenuity to counterbalance her lack of height, my godmother rekindled the greatest lesson in life: when you want to accomplish something, accomplish it. How easy to ask, please stir the spaghetti, I can't reach it. But a kitchen chair gave Aunt Anna height, no excuses.

Several hours later at my father's family in Queens, my mother and her sisters-in-law gather dishes, set tables, prepare salads, and cut bread. In the dining room, my father, with the few men who did not go to war, argue over their favorite boxers, baseball players, and politics. Our two families were incredibly similar. In both cases there were eleven children, and then of course many cousins, so gatherings were crowded and noisy. And, oddly enough, many of my aunts shared the same names with my aunts from my mother's family, carbon copy relatives.

I hear my mother calling.

"Anthony?"

Grandpa, an old man, enters kitchen, limping from arthritis.

"Ciao, Evelina?"

"No, Pa, not you, my son."

Grandpa exits to the backyard.

"Anthony? Anthony? Anthony?"

Two cousins enter the kitchen from opposite directions.

"Aunt Helen, you calling me?"

"No, my son."

"He's upstairs."

My mother comes upstairs, calling.

"Anthony? Anthony?"

As she enters the bedroom, she sees me in my loose-fitting argyle sweater.

"Why didn't you answer me?"

"How am I supposed to know you mean me? Everybody here is named Anthony."

"Shut up before your father hears you."

"You mean he doesn't know we're all named Anthony? Why don't we tell him?"

"Everybody is named after someone else. It's an honor to be named after somebody."

"And we all had to be named after Grandpa?"

She's amused but tries to gain her ground.

"That mouth is gonna get you into trouble. Besides you were named after St. Anthony."

"I want my own name. From now on, call me Eugene."

"Your name is Anthony."

"My name is also Eugene."

"That's only your baptism name."

"Why do I have it, if I can't use it?"

"It's the name God knows you by, no one else."

She could always make me laugh.

"Mom, that's stupid."

"Well someday when you meet Him, ask Him."

That provides a good belly laugh for both of us.

"I named you Anthony for life. You have no choice."

"Then from now on call me Tony."

"Only gangsters are called Tony. Your name's Anthony and that's that."

She starts downstairs, yelling over her shoulder, "Tony's a ridiculous name."

"My name is Tony. When you call me that from now on I'll answer."

As she descends the stairs she tries to win her argument.

"Till the day I die, I'll never call you that. Mark my words!"

I go out to the backyard to my grandfather's huge vegetable garden, but as soon as I arrive I hear Grandma call everyone to dinner, at which point three women yell.

"Annntthhhonnny!"

Several voices, other than mine, could be heard answering the call.

"Coming." "One second." "Be right there."

Grandpa stops his gardening.

"Come on, Anthony, dinner is ready."

I shake my head, in wonder, could they have squeezed one more Anthony into this family?

※

MY MOTHER DIED sixty-seven years later and she never once ever called me Tony. In fact, after my mother was dead, I was having a psychic reading with a woman called Tula. Late into the reading Tula, who had early in the reading told me my mother, father, and sister were in the room with us, began to tell me something.

"Tony..."

Tula stopped speaking and looked to her left where earlier she had established the position of my mother. She spoke to my mother's spirit.

"What?"

Tula listened for my mother's response. Then, with an astonished look Tula said,

"Your mother won't let me call you Tony."

At which point I yelled, "Oh my God, they really are here, aren't they?"

I had never met Tula before, and Tula did not know me or have access to me from anyone else. So, even in the afterlife my mother insists we must mark her words!

❋

AS MY FATHER IS PACKING to return to war from his furlough I ask his advice.

"What should I tell them?"

"Only you can make that decision."

"But they all keep asking. Why do they always want to know what I'm gonna be when I grow up?"

"They know you're good in school and they're interested in you, that's all."

"But I don't know what I'm supposed to tell them."

"When you figure out what you want to do with your life, then you will have an answer to give them."

"I like dancing."

"But dancing, even if you're really good at it, has too many limits. If you go into dancing and you're not good enough to get work, what good is your choice? You don't want that kind of a life."

"How do I find what I do want?"

"Listen, Anthony, you're a bright kid. And you're good in school. One day you'll find the thing in life you like the most that comes easiest to you. Do that, you'll be successful."

As my father took his suitcase and left the room I pondered his simple advice. In the background I could hear the farewells. My father's advice was uncomplicated. Throughout the years I realize how he rarely gave me advice, but when he did it was always exact and applicable to me. His words did not include what would make him happy as a father if I, for instance, would pick the career he hoped for me.

"It's your life Anthony. You have to live it. So, you don't want to pick something to make me happy."

Instead, he advised me.

"Pick the thing in life you like the most that comes easiest to you. Do that, you'll be successful."

Fifteen years later, I found that thing, exactly as he had suggested, as a graduate student in Catholic University's Drama Department when I was directing Patty Mohan and Joy Mills in two scenes from *The Glass Menagerie* and during those rehearsals I knew what came easiest to me, so I chose to become a director for life.

I will share a similar suggestion about my father's valuable advice that saved my life years later. My father would take me into the ocean just before he went to war and hold my hand so I could go with him past the waves, even though my mother was screaming hysterically that I was about to drown. Then he would ask me to stretch out over the water while he placed his right hand under my stomach. From then on he calmly asked me to swim one arm at a time, and put my head into the water with my eyes open and exhale as I went into the water, then inhale as soon as my head came out of the water sideways. And so on. And of course I learned to swim fairly well, enough to enjoy the ocean throughout my life. That is, except one day on Martha's Vineyard in 1981, when Mark McDermott (now known as Dylan), Patricia Clarkson, Eve Ensler, and I hid our rental car in the brush along a beach in Gay Head on Martha's Vineyard. Then, despite a huge 'Do Not Trespass' sign we snuck onto the empty beach.

Mark and I went into the water, and we were instantly in trouble. The riptide, the size of the waves, the cracking of those waves, and the enormous slippery boulders in that ocean were beyond either of our abilities. Mark struggled between the big boulders, falling from one to the other until he found a way out of the water and walked up to wake Eve and Patty. He was quite dazed as he walked out of the sea.

Once I saw that Mark was back on the sand, I stupidly thought good, now I can swim because I don't have to worry about Mark, so I turned to the ocean and was immediately pulled way out by a riptide as if a rope was tied to my left ankle. It dragged me fast and furious into freezing water where the waves kept breaking so heavily my shoulder froze. I then noticed the only other man in the water not too far from me, struggling as well.

My breath became very short, but I fortunately recalled my father's advice.

"If ever you find yourself in dangerous ocean conditions, lay on your side and let the ocean take you wherever it will. Once you are in that position, figure out the pattern of the waves. As soon as you can understand the pattern, then begin to swim back to shore, stopping and lying on your side each time it's necessary."

As I did this, Patty and Eve, concerned by what Mark told them, came with Mark to the end of the shore to watch as I managed to swim back to shore. As soon as I was safe, we all turned and looked for that man, who was nowhere to be seen. We waited for about twenty minutes and then drove to the sheriff's office to admit where we had been and to report a drowning.

Thank you, Dad, there are no limits to good advice. His words might only have been about mundane things like drowning, but with my skill for metaphors and subtexts I was able to take his words as far as my imagination would go, into an honest trust that you can do just about anything if you relax and figure it out, quietly and without fear. Oddly, the moment the television news announced John Kennedy Jr., his wife, and her sister were lost in a plane going to Hyannis Port, I knew they drowned in the vortex of those same waters I had struggled to save my life.

What is weird is that my father was never in my face. He watched but rarely intruded. He always seemed amused that I functioned on my own. I can only recall about half a dozen pieces of advice he ever gave me, and they all always paid off when the time arrived for me to use them.

The night my father completed his furlough and had gone back to the war our bedroom is re-inhabited by Theresa, my mother, and myself. While my mother and Theresa are in their beds, I frantically search the closet for the booty my father gave me, but they are nowhere to be found. My mother tries to stop me.

"Come to bed. You can look again tomorrow."

"Where did you hide them?"

"I don't know what you're talking about."

I climb into bed, but I am not about to give in.

Tell me what you did with my souvenirs."

"I lost them."

"Daddy gave them to me."

"Keep looking for them. You'll find them."

"You threw them away, didn't you?"

"Your father didn't know what he was doing. Go to bed."

"I want an altar."

"An altar? What are you talking about?"

"The ones in church."

"Only priests have altars. What's wrong with you?"

Theresa rarely misses an opportunity.

"He's crazy. I told you."

"I'm gonna get an altar."

"Where did you ever get such an idea?"

"From church. The priest has one."

"He's a priest."

"Well I want one."

"Over my dead body. Now go to sleep."

"You can't stop me."

"What's this thing about an altar?"

"Grandma wants me to be a priest."

"My mother?"

"Daddy's."

"Who the hell does she think she is telling you to be a priest? Waste your life for what?"

"She says the family needs one."

"A priest? What a thing to tell a kid. If she wants a priest, let her have another baby."

Finally revenge, an altar, in exchange for war booty.

❋

I'VE BEEN SITTING in the headmaster's office for about two hours. The secretary is filing papers.

"Maybe you should take a walk."

"What if I miss him?"

"He won't be here for hours. Really."

"Where can I walk?"

"You might go out to the football field. But you can't go upstairs."

"May I leave my coat here?"

"It's cold out."

"I won't be long."

I feel my coat left on this chair will maintain my presence.

As I leave the office I once again find myself in this spotless hallway, wondering what it must have been like throughout those generations of traditions, how many fathers and uncles walked through this hallway and now wait at home for their sons and grandsons to return for dinner every night to compare what Prep is like to the days when they studied here. My family also has great traditions, but they're mostly about food.

I locate the auditorium/gymnasium and walk in. I am alone. I sit on one of the open bleachers and little by little recall the day one year ago when I took the entrance exam in this very room. In my memory I'm suddenly surrounded by hundreds of thirteen-year-old boys sitting nervously, preparing to compete to enter this school. Jesuits dressed in plain black slacks with black cassocks, no ornaments of any kind, usher applicants to every available seat. I'm sitting about midway in the auditorium, wearing my argyle sweater. Lay teachers wear professorial black robes over their suits. One priest places metal chairs against a little table, then calls to the entrance of the auditorium.

"Paul, I can take four more."

Paul turns out to be another priest, about fifty-five years old, at the doorway with the excess applicants. He sends over four boys and shouts back.

"Three thousand, counting all classrooms."

"We'll make it. Send another two."

Two other Jesuits are setting up a long table against the front edge of the stage. They indicate with their fingers for twelve boys. Paul sends them twelve. Tables are also set up on the stage itself. I am witnessing unity and cooperation. Despite the overwhelming number of students competing for a chance to come to this school, these priests and teachers carry out their tasks with calm and ease that makes this large task seem ordinary.

The tall athletic priest in his thirty's addresses us.

"Good morning. My name is John Culkin. We will begin the test in a few minutes, so let's get ready. Make certain you have elbowroom, about two yards. You need space to think, and to place your papers, rulers and erasers."

Fr. Paul, amused, calls out.

"John, one yard will have to do."

"Oh! Of course."

Fr. Paul explains.

"Two yards John is seventy-two inches."

Then Fr. Paul speaks to us.

"Don't worry. He teaches Greek."

We all laugh, and even Fr. Culkin is happy about this joke at his expense.

"Fr. Paone keeps me humble. Okay, one yard. But the point is that you must be comfortable in order to do your best work. We want you to relax so you can think clearly. Don't get nervous or intimidated by the questions. Read each question at least twice. If you have no answer for it, move on to a question that you can answer. The sooner you solve the problems that are easy for you, the sooner you can return to those questions that seem too difficult."

The priest who set the four chairs at the table tells us.

"Check to see that your pen is filled with ink, your pencils are sharp, your ruler is ready, and your eraser is cleaned."

An applicant raises his hand.

"Can I sharpen my pencils?"

Fr. "Paul" Paone answers.

"Come over here. If you need to sharpen your pencils during the tests, raise your hand for permission. Do not speak to each other during these exams, or we will have to ask you to leave."

Fr. Culkin continues, "I'll be moderating the morning and afternoon sessions with you. There will be five hours of testing, three this morning and two this afternoon. That's a good deal of sitting and thinking, so before you begin, stand up. Now! Everybody up!"

Then he asks the faculty of priests and lay teachers to open all the windows. And they do.

"Now breathe. Deep. Exhale. Breathe. Exhale. Touch your toes. Up. Down. Come on. Up. Down. Now jump up and down a couple of times. Faster. Lift those knees to your chest. Shake your head and let it fall down. Lift your shoulders and drop them a few times. Now stand still. Relax! Breathe slowly through your nose. Hold it. Exhale through your mouth. Again: breathe, hold, exhale. Now just stand there for a few seconds, close your eyes, relax. Until the bell rings, just relax. Receive the grace of the Holy Spirit to do your best work."

A silence spreads throughout the auditorium. I can feel the spring breeze fill the room. I closed my eyes, smiling for I found the alternate world I am looking for. Brooklyn Prep. All I have to do is pass the test in the top percentage.

I snap out of my reverie when I hear the voice of a priest facing me.

"What are you doing out of class?"

"I don't go to school here."

"What are you doing here then?"

"Just looking."

"Why?"

"No reason."

"No reason?"

"No."

"What's your name?"

"Anthony."

"I'm Mr. Ryan."

"The headmaster's assistant."

"How did you know?"

"His secretary told me."

"Sounds like an odd thing for a secretary to talk about."

"She calls you Fr. Ryan."

"I will be. Jesuits are called mister until ordination."

"Oh."

"First thirteen years as mister. Then father. I have two more years."

"She said I could walk around."

"Go ahead."

"But that I can't go upstairs."

"Well, you can go upstairs and peak around, quietly. No noise in the hallways is permitted during class that's all. Just don't run into Fr. Engles."

"Why?"

"You'll know why if you meet him. He's our prefect of discipline, here to maintain school rules. And believe me he does."

"Sounds scary."

"I've been afraid of him for years."

We laugh together.

"What'll I do if he stops me?"

"Pray. God is merciful."

We laugh louder. What a great guy!

"Can I help? Do you want something?"

"No, thank you."

"Nothing?"

"Well, I'm waiting to see Fr. Watson."

"He's at a conference."

"In New York, I know."

"You probably know more of what's going on here today than anyone else."

"God, I hope not."

This amuses Mr. Ryan.

"Since I'm his assistant, perhaps I can help. What do you want?"

"I want to talk to Fr. Watson."

"And no one else?"

"Well, I really want to talk to him."

"You sure?"

"Yes."

"Okay, nice meeting you."

Mr. Ryan walks away. I go outside to the fields. There are several classes working out in calisthenics, track, football, and three singular track guys jogging with a coach using a stopwatch to time their pace. A teacher announces the end of the gym session and students rush by me back into the building. I follow them down into the locker room where they shower and change back into their full clothing. I am amazed at how quickly they dress back into their shirts, ties, jackets, pants, and shoes. No substitutes. Obviously they must retain a dress code. I decide to brave the upstairs as the class bell rings and as gym students rush past me to their next class.

Everything this morning at Prep is adding up to what my mother would insist will "Break your heart," since everything that is happening is making me really want to be a student here. The stakes are higher than when I arrived at nine a.m. There are many ways to break your heart. To find the alternate world you are looking for and then fail to enter it could be catastrophic. I had already felt the pangs of suffering, sometimes for my own battles, sometimes because I stood by and watched people I love suffer and could do nothing about it. I did not need to fail this battle.

For instance, one winter day after school, Aunt Anna and I were cooking, or so I like to fantasize. She was standing on a kitchen chair stirring a huge pot of spaghetti sauce with meats. I was placing cans of food, chocolates, underwear, gloves, and socks into four cardboard boxes. These were care packages my family sent to my father and uncles to remind them of home. In my family, food definitely was the root of all love and fortunately Aunt Anna, Grandma, my mother, and in fact each of my aunts, were all great cooks.

Suddenly the sound of our apartment buzzer scares us. We rarely hear that buzzer since the family enters with keys, but today it has an ominous sound. Aunt Anna climbs off her chair, presses for the outside front door to open, and walks down our hallway to open our apartment door. I follow by her side.

"Western Union! Alfredo Sbarra?"

Trembling, Aunt Anna answers him.

"He's not here. That's my father. He's at work."

"Can you sign for him?"

"Yes."

She signs, closes the door, and rushes back to the kitchen. In the kitchen Aunt Anna shakes as she opens the telegram. She grabs her chest.

"Oh my God, Andy! Oh dear mother of God, they shot my little brother. Uncle Andy has been shot."

Finally war was here.

"Oh God, Anthony, pray that he'll be all right. He's in a hospital in France."

Then she weeps, soft and personal, with no embarrassment. It was her relief.

I ask, "Why do we have war?"

"To kill people."

"I mean what are we fighting for?"

"Peace. It's all so stupid."

"Is there no other way?"

"How do I know? It's enough to break your heart. Take the cans of sardines out of the bag and divide them in the boxes. We've got to let the men know we care."

She leans over to baste chicken and potatoes with onions, garlic, and peas in the oven.

"Wait'll Grandpa and the family come home from work. Anthony, pray to end this war. Tell God to put some sense into everyone's brainless heads."

This was the impetus I needed now to save the world. I would end the war. My mother forfeited her rights over me when she threw my war booty away. So I have the right to declare war by building my altar, to tell God to put sense into everyone's brainless head and end this war. That night, in my pajamas before I go to bed I go into my aunts' bedroom, and with the help of Aunt Gracie, the family saint, I make an altar by draping a sheet over a small wooden box for the tabernacle and down the top and sides of a low dresser. I add candles, a statue of the Lady of Prague, the crucified Christ, and dry flowers in a vase. Aunt Gracie enters surreptitiously from fear of what we're doing. Radio war news flows in from the parlor. She brings me a crystal stem glass, a bottle of Grandpa's wine with a small amount at the bottom, and three United Biscuits.

"Don't let this drop. You can use it for a chalice. Here are three biscuits for the wafer. Don't ever tell your mother I did this or she'll kill me. I brought you more candles from church. Anthony, are you gonna become a priest?"

"I don't think so. Where can I get real flowers?"

"I don't know if you're supposed to make an altar if you're not gonna be a Priest."

As I place the chalice and biscuits, I echo grandma.

"God understands, Aunt Gracie, don't worry."

An air raid siren begins, which always creates fear in this family. They behave as if we're being bombed. Aunt Dottie shouts down the hallway.

"Get the lights, hurry!"

I hear my mother from the other end of the apartment.

"Lower the shades!"

Aunt Josie opens the door of this bedroom. She is hysterical.

"The lights! What are you two doing in here?"

Aunt Gracie is scared.

"Oh my God! Anthony, quick, let's go!"

Josie runs off. Gracie lowers the shades, turns off lights in the bedroom. It is now pitch black. Aunt Gracie starts losing her breath.

"I can't see anything. Anthony, are you all right? Josie, are you here? Where's Anna? Someone protect Anna."

I light a match.

"Relax, Aunt Gracie, it's just air raid practice."

"We should be with the others."

I hold the match while she finds her way to the door. She joins Dottie, who's passing with a lighted candle and screaming hysterically.

"Hurry! This one's real. I can feel it."

Gracie and Dottie run off, scaring each other. They're too frightened to realize I've stayed behind. I close the bedroom door and light the candles, which flicker against the cross. I clasp my hands and talk to God against the sound of sirens.

"When I sing, they laugh. When I dance, they laugh more. When I ask questions, they say shut up. I can't find answers. And I don't know how to end this war. I don't even know what war is. What is it?"

I wait for God to answer.

"Tell me what to do."

The act of prayer is dynamic because of the idealism involved. Of course, some of the fun is playing a priest because you assume a priest can save the world. Prayer is hoping. You are positive that God is listening. You have identified a problem, detected things that should be corrected, and are dealing with the suffering of others.

When word spread throughout the apartment that I was saying Mass Theresa disowned me.

"I told you he's mad. No one listens to me."

She pleaded with everyone to believe her. It was clear they were ready to agree. After dinner was the perfect time for me to perform services, since the family were cleaning fanatics and were scrubbing every spot from the kitchen and the dining room. My mother stepped aside since she was disgusted with me. Aunt Gracie was my only parishioner. I prayed for my father and my uncles. I wanted to see them again. I prayed for Grandma and Grandpa to live forever. I prayed when our dog, Queenie, was giving birth, though Aunt Josie kept calling Queenie *puttana* because she roamed the neighborhood until she was pregnant twice before. Josie did not feel Queenie needed any prayers to do this. But I prayed for her anyway since I did not know the facts of life. And I prayed when the sirens sounded during the blackouts, using on these occasions, small votive candles.

Though World War II broke out in Poland the year I was born, it took several years to reach my family and when it did, I have to confess, it was the best thing that ever happened to me. I had completed questions about birth, but when my father and uncles became soldiers, and my mother responded with utter hostility to Nazis, I had my second question. What is war? This question was complex and compound, so it thrilled me. Then of course we moved in with the family and I was the center of attention. And that was fun.

The blackouts that would frighten the family would excite the hell out of me. I loved hearing the sirens and those disembodied voices in the night shouting from the street to turn our lights off. We had special black shades that covered our front and back windows, and we turned our lights off as well, so we became hermetically sealed. It made the family feel safe from attack. They assumed that if the enemy couldn't see us, they couldn't kill us.

It involved me in the war. My father and I were fighting the war together. Europe, they told me, was over the ocean. I now had an uncle who survived the enemy's bullet and I had blackouts to bring me into the war. More importantly, the fact that blackouts were only playacting taught me how truthful playacting is. Since the family refused to answer my question "What is war?," blackouts gave me the answer. For whether the enemy was actually attacking, or whether my family's fear made an imaginary attack real, the panic they experienced was huge.

❋

I CLIMB A BACK STAIRCASE to Prep's second floor, which is quiet except for the sound of a teacher's voice coming from an open classroom. I tiptoe behind the opened door, through the crack of which I can see the back of the priest sitting on the top of one of the desks.

In the background the class faces the priest.

"How many of you studied with the nuns?"

Half of the students raise their hands.

"Brothers?"

More raise hands.

"Lay teachers?"

A few hands.

"Fuck."

The class stirs. My eyes widen.

"What? What? Speak up."

One student speaks.

"What you said."

"What did I say?"

"You know."

The priest continues feigned innocence.

"What?"

"I can't say it."

The priest helps out.

"Fuck?"

The class stirs again, shocked. I know real life, so I know such words and can enjoy how this priest is teasing his class. The student answers father's question.

"Yes, of course."

"Nuns?"

"Yes."

So the priest explains.

"The good nuns feel an obligation to teach children, so they make things simple. We teach men. There is nothing wrong with the word 'you,' or the word 'fuck.' It is the intention that matters. We should not expect nuns to tell you this, since they want to make you as pure as possible and they certainly don't want you to go home and tell your family such a taboo is okay, so they teach what is acceptable."

One student calls out.

"Why is it such a taboo then?"

Father eggs the student on.

"What?"

"You know."

"What?"

The student complies.

"Fuck."

Father asks him.

"That feel good?"

"Very."

The class laughs.

"Because people remain ignorant and don't think for themselves. They become conformists. So when a society creates a taboo, everyone falls in line. I am not telling you to use such a word since you know how people feel about it, but I am recommending that you investigate such a word and scrutinize it. Then you will discover that most times people call out that word to curse someone and their intention to curse someone is what makes the word wrong. At Prep we want you to think for yourselves, but first you have to do what the Greeks believed. They call it *gnothi seauton*.

I swing around to the other side to see the blackboard as the priest writes *gnothi seauton*.

"This means to Know Thyself. We cannot learn anything if we don't know who we are. When we know ourselves, we know the entire universe, because the universe is made from the same essential being as we are. What makes it hard to know ourselves is that we are born in medias res."

He pauses again and writes that on the board in medias res.

"In medias res means in the middle of things. We enter life surrounded by family and a world in motion. Who am I? Why am I here? What am I supposed to do with my life? Our educational plan covers the entire person and tries to answers questions so you learn how to live your lives."

He writes again on the board as he talks to his class.

"*Sanitas. Scientias. Sanctitas.* Body. Mind. Soul. To become individuals you have to be healthy in body, mind, and soul. To do this you have to cleanse those things that have become embedded within you. Investigate early memories where you form prejudices, which now hold you back by cluttering your soul. Take out a pen and jot down the first memory you have of some prejudice you feel. Let's see if we can erase it. As freshmen you will have four years with us to solve these problems."

Wow! Answers! I feel my blood boil.

Elated, I move to the staircase behind two young Jesuits climbing the stairs ahead of me.

One tells the other, "Paone spent eight months behind the iron curtain in a jail cell with four nuns and three other priests. Soldiers would rape the nuns, then kick the other priests in their groins until they passed out. I read his diary till four."

"He returns to the missions as soon as his health is better."

Good God. Jesuits live in the world I crave.

※

AFTER SCHOOL ONE DAY, I'm hanging around Aunt Anna's kitchen. She is cooking while my mother beads jewelry for her job on the kitchen table. I'm standing near the window, and on its ledge I'm mixing spices and milk into a colorful bowl while I sing.

". . . birds fly over the rainbow, way up high. Why, then, oh why can't I?"

My mother does not appreciate the quality of my voice.

"You're giving me a headache. You sing like a broken record."

But by now I'd learned to forge past insults.

"If happy little bluebirds fly, beyond the rainbow . . ."

"What a pain in the ass you are. Do you know that?"

Mom and I are still angry at each other because of my souvenirs from Europe and my altar, which she sacrilegiously dismantled. So I stop singing to confront her.

"Do you know you're a pain in the ass too?"

She thinks she can outrank me.

"Who do you think you're talking to?"

I look around the kitchen.

"You're the one I have been talking to, haven't I?"

Amused by me, as usual, she adds.

"Wise guy! Keep your voice down. Grandma's not feeling well. What are you mixing?"

"I'm cooking."

"What are you cooking?"

"Dinner."

"Throw it away for God's sakes."

"We're gonna eat it."

"Well, you eat it first. If you're still alive, the rest of us will eat it."

At this point I rub my eyes to deal with an itch and begin to scream in agony.

"Ouch . . . oh . . . wow . . . it hurts."

"What do you have in that bowl?"

She takes me to the sink and leans my head backwards so she can pour water into my eyes.

Aunt Anna is at the stove, cooking.

"That's too cold."

Aunt Anna asks.

"What happened?"

"He burned his eyes."

Anna goes to the window ledge and reads back to us.

"Black pepper, red pepper, crushed pepper . . . paprika, no wonder."

My mother always takes advantage of trouble to win a point.

"Now maybe you'll learn to keep your mind on school."

BROOKLYN ODYSSEY 59

But Aunt Anna is more generous.
"How do you feel?"
"It burns."
She comforts.
"It'll go away. Go inside while we cook."
As I exit my mother taunts by singing, mockingly.
"Somewhere over the rainbow . . ."
I run to the parlor, turn on the radio, and dance with an imaginary partner, singing along.
". . . *and finally found the somebody who could make me be true, and could make me be blue and even be glad, just to be sad thinking of you.*"
My mother arrives and watches from the doorway.
"*Some others I've seen, might . . .*"
She turns the radio off.
"Why do you keep wishing for things you can never have?"
The roar of a plane can be heard over our apartment.
"You'll break your heart. You hear me?"
I rush to the window to look up at the plane.
"I wish I was on that plane."
"You don't even know where it's going."
"Well I know it's not landing here."
"You would rather be anywhere but here? That doesn't make me feel so good."
"I want to see things."
"You want all the wrong things in life. Settle down as soon as possible. That's my advice to you. Your head is too big for such a little boy. Our people work hard. We don't get things handed to us on a silver platter."
"What does that mean?"
"We have bigger problems than worrying about dancing or traveling around the world. That's not so hard to understand."
"Like what?"
"Stop thinking of yourself. What have I raised here?"
"Like what? That's not such a hard question to understand, is it?"
"Like a war, you idiot. People are suffering all over the world but you're only interested in having fun? Where did you come from? Huh?"

"Don't you ever want to travel and see things?"

"The world is the same wherever you go. Whatta you think? You get off a plane and things are different?"

"Why is the world the same everywhere? Something must be different."

"Let me give you some simple advice. You'd be better off just to sit quietly in a corner, close your eyes, and thank God for the life you have. There are people struggling to survive, who don't even have a bed to sleep in at night. Some are living with bombs over their heads."

"Let's help them."

"Oh, you're gonna solve everybody's problems? My helpless son."

"Why not?"

"Anthony, take care of your own life. One less person causing trouble in this world is good enough. When this war ends and you're older, you'll see what I'm talking about. Meantime keep your nose clean. Your father is away in this crazy war. That's enough for me to worry about. Do your homework and do well in school. Make us proud of you. That will be enough for you to accomplish. Just stop all your daydreaming. It will only break your heart to want things you can't have. Do you hear me?"

"There must have been something in life you dreamed about when you were young."

"When I was a few years older than you are now I was working in a factory."

"Why?"

"Aunt Rosie, Uncle Alfred, and I were the oldest. That's why. And Grandma and Grandpa worked too, but none of us made much money, just enough to keep the family together. There were seven younger brothers and sisters, remember. And Aunt Anna spent two years with a cast over her entire body because of her illness. We had to pay for all of that."

"Did you ever dream about anything else?"

"When I saw Myrna Loy I was eight years old and thought I looked liked her, maybe I could make movies."

"Did you ever try?"

"Don't you listen? I worked in a factory and that was that."

"But I don't have seven younger brothers and sisters."

"But if it's not one thing, it's another. There's talent too you know. You think Fred Astaire learned how to dance? He's a natural, so that's what he did."

"You mean I can't learn?"

"Not the way you think. And you could waste your life trying to be something that you weren't born for. Studying is really for you. You ask too many questions for me, but teachers are happy with you. School's your thing, Anthony."

She left the room and left me thinking. If the world was so terrible, why could we not fix it? And if I was interested in helping the world, why would it be better for me to sit in a corner quietly and do nothing? None of this made sense to me. All I was asking to do was to do something. I was imprisoned in an apartment filled with love and good food but no connection to life beyond. Yet my father was off in a war to help the world I was not permitted to investigate. I don't know if this was one of the seeds that helped me later in life to realize paradox, that things are not what they seem to be. I should sympathize with people who were struggling rather than think about myself, but the best way to behave was then to concentrate on myself rather than do anything for the people who were struggling. Paradox?

❊

I AM NOW ON THE TOP FLOOR of Prep, looking into a chemistry lab, watching experiments. There are rocks on many tables and the students seem to be studying them with great intensity. I walk closer to the next room where I can hear other interesting teaching though I cannot make out what this class is. The elderly priest speaks to one student.

"Heat, its conductor force? That's not hard, Mr. Carney. Not unless you spend afternoons running track and not doing your homework."

"We had a meet, Father."

"When you flunk out of school and your parents ask me why, I'll tell them you had a meet."

"I get your point."

"Let's have a round of applause. Mr. Carney gets my point."

The class applauds.

"Now perhaps we can return to heat conductors. Mr. Robinson . . . ?"

※

OUR BEDROOM IS DARK and away from the rest of the family. It is the middle of the night. My mother is not with us. I hear whispering down the hallway. Theresa is in her bed. I get up and start to leave.

"Stay here." Theresa commands. "You'll only be in the way."

But I don't take orders from her, so I walk through the darkened apartment to the dim hallway, as Josie and Anna are at the front door with a doctor.

"I'll be back in the morning."

Down the hallway I see Grandpa sitting in the kitchen, alone. The doctor leaves. Aunt Josie sees me in the shadows.

"Anthony, get to bed. This is no time for you to be awake."

Aunt Anna assures her.

"He'll be all right."

Josie and Anna enter Grandma's bedroom. While the door is ajar, I can see my mother, Aunt Dottie, and Aunt Gracie changing Grandma's bedclothes. The door closes. I walk to the kitchen. Grandpa is sitting in his chair at the porcelain table, lifeless. I go to the pantry, take a large onion, and bring it to the table. At this point the sound of women crying begins. Grandpa grabs me and hugs me like a teddy bear. We both know.

※

TWO DAYS LATER in the funeral home Dottie, Gracie, Josie, and Rosie are accepting sympathy from relatives, neighbors and friends. Some wear yarmulkes. While Aunt Rosie introduces neighbors to the family, I ask my mother what I should do. This is my first death.

"Go up to the coffin and say a prayer for grandma. You can kiss her if you want to. We all do that."

So I walk to Grandma's coffin, bless myself as I kneel, and kiss Grandma's cheek. I rush back to my mother.

"Grandma tastes like cement."

Without flinching my mother responds.

"That's from the formaldehyde."

"What's that?"

"In the funeral parlor they don't want the body to deteriorate. So they use formaldehyde. You have to learn to live with death, Anthony, whether you like it or not. That's what life is all about. Grandma brought so much life to this earth; her death should not be offensive to anyone."

"What happens to her now."

"God takes her back."

"Where?"

"Heaven, you know that from catechism."

"But how's He do that?"

"He does, that's all."

"Well how?"

"Those are mysteries, Anthony, no one knows but God."

As she goes to the door to greet members of my father's family, I call out.

"Someone must know."

There are many people who believe children should be saved from such "hideous" events as the death of a grandmother, or death period. But thanks to my family, particularly my mother, I was invited to accept life in all of its configurations. While in college I enjoyed skiing whenever I could afford to go. My enjoyment was in some way the result of that death experience, for I learned early in life you cannot do something as dangerous as skiing if you do not know how to fall, or living if you do not know about death. So on my first trip to North Conway in New Hampshire, my accomplished ski friends took me to the top of the mountain. The three trails had the same ominous notation printed on a board and nailed to their trees: 'Intermediate to Expert'. The one my friends chose said it was the 'Rattlesnake', so they skidded down out of my sight. Naturally, I was scared. So I started to follow them down the mountain (now remember I had never been on skis before) and immediately threw myself sideways so I would fall and learn what happens to those enormous skis when you go down. Then I stood up, tried a few feet further and threw myself down sideways on the other side, and so on until I reached the bottom. Then I immediately went back to the top and repeated this for several more trips until that afternoon when I began to ski down the Rattlesnake with the ability to stay on my skis the entire trip. I had learned to fall, so I could begin to ski, for now I knew if trouble was ahead, like a tree in my way, I would throw myself away from it and save my life. Ever since Grandma's death I have always known I will die. The result has been a wonderful free existence where I have dedicated my life to life, that is, to living as well and as fully as possible, because I already know about death, the falling. I clearly thank my mother for this life lesson.

In the funeral parlor Aunt Rosie introduces relatives I have never met to neighbors. The husband is wearing a yarmulke.

"I want you to meet my mother's sister Mary and her husband, Joey Kaufman."

I notice my Aunt Anna sitting next to Grandpa in front of the coffin. I walk to the back of their chairs and stand with a hand on each of their necks. My grandfather never really spoke so to say on this day he was speechless would make no sense. But what made sense was the picture of him sitting in the pain of loss next to his crippled daughter and both of them were totally helpless. I kept discovering my own helplessness. I could feel sorrow for others but I had no solutions.

I walked back to my mother when Grandma's "Little scrawny Irish priest with the whisky nose" gathers the family to say the rosary. The relatives with the yarmulkes stand to the side and do not join in the prayers. This makes me curious.

"Why, Mom?"

"Because they're Jewish. They are part of our family but not part of our religion. They have their own religion."

Some forty years later I was directing James Whitmore and Audra Lindley in Bill Gibson's play *Handy Dandy*. Several weeks before I flew to California to begin rehearsals, I was interviewed by telephone with one of LA's local newspapers, so there was no picture attached. When I arrived at the Pasadena Playhouse, the receptionist told me there had been a call for me from someone who read the article and wondered if he was my cousin. His name, she said, was Joey Kaufman, so I asked for the note with his telephone number and she blushed.

"What's the matter?"

"Well, he wasn't certain if you were his cousin, and because his name seemed different from yours I thought it was just some crank reading an article."

She assumed Kaufman/Giordano could not be related, you know Jewish/Catholic. Well, years after that incident my mother was dying from congestive heart failure, and to cheer her up I tried to tell her this story.

"You didn't call him back? How can you do that to Joey?"

"Mom, the girl didn't keep his telephone number."

"Why not?"

"She thought we couldn't be cousins, you know Kaufman/Giordano."

"I don't understand."

"She figured he was Jewish and I was Catholic, so we couldn't be related."

At that point my mother went into as much rage as her weakened body could afford and pointed to Heaven with her dangerous fist.

"What business is it of hers who our cousins are? Tell her to mind her own business."

My mother never needed to be part of the women's movement of the seventies and eighties. In fact I used to say to those women who were a part of it, "Haven't you ever met my mother?"

❋

THROUGH THE OPEN DOOR I can see that the Jesuit teaching Greek is the same one from my entrance exam, the one who brought grades to the secretary this morning, Fr. Culkin. He's writing on the blackboard.

"Scylla and Charybdis. If Odysseus turns his boat left, the power of that monster, Scylla, will overturn his boat and devour his men, her six great mouths each demanding to be fed. That's Scylla! If he turns the boat right, whirling Charybdis will crack the boat against the floor of the sea and smash boat and crew to smithereens. There is no escape. What's that called?"

One student raises his hand.

"Yes, Mr. Brennan?"

"Dramatic tension."

"Right. And the greatness of Odysseus is measured by . . . what?"

Three students raise their hands.

"Mr. Azzarto?"

"His ability to get his men out alive."

"Exactly, the dilemma of Scylla and Charybdis, how to get out alive. You will meet them many times before you die. Mr. McMillan?'

"When we meet them, what if we cannot get out from them?"

"We fail. Daily life challenges us to own our personal odyssey."

Fr. Culkin comes to the doorway, sees me, and stares into my eyes. I stare in return, and then, rather than shooing me away, Fr. Culkin includes me in the lesson by relating sometimes to me; at other times to his class. He has one of those personalities that demonstrate curiosity in who I could possibly be, standing in a hallway of Prep, clearly an outsider peeking in. After all, he kind of knows me, since we met in the office earlier. He speaks as if to me.

"Everything you do in your life adds up, even when you are unaware of it. Each experience helps to make you what you are. You may not recall each experience, but if you succeed along the way, those successes rest within you and help you toward further success. The strongest people become leaders who complete their odysseys and then lead the way for others. That's the purpose of a good education. Put simply, you beat Scylla and Charybdis. Something to think about, huh?"

Culkin observes me walk away, then turns to the class and I can hear his final thoughts.

"Okay, for tonight read through Epis. 9, 'The Great Battle in the Hall.' Let's look at line 2000, *olethov peipat'eq^npto*. Since *meipap* also means the end of the rope, Homer's idiom can easily be captured in English: the noose of death had been drawn tight."

People with answers were appearing everywhere like clear water from a mountain stream.

❋

WHEN WORLD WAR II ENDED, our neighbors celebrated with a victory block party. Thanks to war, the neighborhood became a family! But my mood at usual ran contrary to everyone else. My father's return was bittersweet as my mother joyfully reported, "We'll move to an apartment."

I felt so much a part of this household that her good news could only meet my deaf ears. On one hand, I wanted my future. Now that my father had returned, this move to our own apartment will give me freedom. On the other hand, Grandpa and Aunt Anna were exhausted from the trials of the war and the death of Grandma. I wanted to stay with them. I began to realize that the suffering felt in remote anticipation is much greater than the awful experience itself, so those who worried, helplessly at home, aged themselves in the process. To the men, the war simply was over. They could return and move on with their lives, filled with adventurous stories. Clearly, just by imagining the war, my mother and her family had been horrified and their imaginations of this would remain deep in their psyche, for the cost of the war had been emotionally billed. These people I loved so much had shared a cross, which had snapped their collective spine. Now I hated whatever the war was about, and wondered why we needed wars. I longed for a world that could enjoy the innocence and sweetness of the Sbarras. But my mother had been embarrassed long enough, and certainly my father couldn't live off of anyone so we would most certainly move.

The day of the block party begins at sunrise on an empty street around the corner from us, with my father and Uncles Andy, Willie, and Alfred, stacking cases of beer and soda in iced chests, neighbors setting up a bandstand and preparing tables for food. People are hanging wreaths, ribbons, balloons, confetti traps to fall on cue, and red, white, and blue decorations and flags to dress up the entire block. As the bandstand is being created, the street is cleaned so we will dance in the streets.

My uncles are having a good old time busting each other's balls. Uncle Andy teases Uncle Willie.

"You didn't get to first base before the war."

"You dirty dog. Wait'll next summer. I'm gonna pitch for the other team."

"Vinnie! Willie is pitching against us. How can we lose?"

Uncle Willie defends himself.

"You skunk. Let's go to the park and hit a few. We'll see who still has it." Andy teases.

"Remember my purple heart."

Uncle Alfred explains to the others.

"We're never gonna live down that purple-heart. You must have found some nurse to lie for you to get it."

In the apartment my mother, Anna, and Dottie prepare huge pans of chicken cacciatore, fried veal cutlets, pepper and sausages, and baked eggplants. Josie makes homemade pizzas and brings them onto the roof adjoining the kitchen window where Grandpa sits alone with our dog, Queenie, at his feet. Perhaps he is thanking God for sending the men home. Or perhaps he is thinking of Grandma. He is such a silent man, who suffers in private. We'll never know. Aunt Gracie makes large bowls of macaroni and potato salads.

Anna is despondent.

"Momma would have loved this."

Then she leaves the kitchen. The women nod in agreement.

On the large oval table in the dining room, Theresa makes hundreds of sandwiches. And on the chests in the dining room Anna's baked cookies, pies, and cakes are cooling. I wander into the living room where the radio is playing.

"I'll be seeing you in all the old familiar places."

Aunt Anna enters and watches me dance in my fashion.

"I miss her, Anthony. Who ever thought?"

I realize that all her worrying for the lives of my uncles and father broke my Aunt Anna's heart. She asks me.

"What's Grandpa gonna do without her?"

I'm only a kid, so I answer as a kid.

"Now the war's over. It'll be okay."

"I don't know what to do."

"What do you mean?"

"You'll all be gone. Aunt Gracie and Aunt Josie are young women. They don't need to take care of me all their lives."

"But you take care of everybody."

"They pay the bills. I'm in their way."

Aunt Anna was feeling awkward because in this family, regardless of their economic struggles, they always paid their way. The jobs were insignificant, but each person brought home something for the expense of food, rent, clothes, school, and doctors. Aunt Anna had the skills of the perfect homemaker, but going out into the world and earning a few dollars gave the others an importance she didn't feel.

Once, many years later, I was asked to speak at the disabled actors committee at the Actors Equity theatrical union. As I walked from my apartment off Central Park on that chilly morning, I realized I didn't even know what the disabled actors committee was or why it existed. When I arrived and sat down in this very large assembly room, I continued to wonder until the first person arrived. He was a well-built blind man in his forties led by a huge seeing-eye dog. Though there was no one else in the room at the time, and though there were at least thirty empty seats surrounding several board tables that were placed in a square, the dog brought his blind master around the longest semi-circle to the seat next to mine and when the blind man sat next to me the dog sat on my feet. I introduced myself and vice versa. Then a skinny man in a wheelchair arrived with legs all twisted. He sat across from us and introduced himself and we in return introduced ourselves. Then others arrived who were deaf, crippled in other ways. Other people entered who were translators for the deaf.

My heart was pounding because now I knew what the disabled actors committee was and who its members were. But I had no idea what I was supposed to say. Then I was introduced as a director who was here to discuss how to get acting jobs for members of this committee. Instantly I flashed back to my Aunt Anna. The first thing I told these actors is what I experienced coming here this morning, worrying that I did not know what this committee was all about and certainly I had no idea what to say until the dog sat on my feet, where he remained the entire time as if he was my anchor to stop me from leaving. I then told them to change the title of their committee. I told them it was nearly impossible for able-bodied actors to find work. To publicize the notion that one should cast a disabled actor is to frighten directors. I said there are fifty million people (now probably one hundred million) with handicaps in America, and as actors you are more capable of representing those fifty million than anyone else.

Surprisingly, they applauded, though to this day they never changed the title of the committee. In any case, we then discussed how they could in fact create plays and musicals indigenous to themselves. I never told them about Aunt Anna because that was not part of their acting needs, but I secretly know that because of my Aunt Anna I have never once viewed a handicapped person as "disabled."

To cure her sadness I invited Aunt Anna outside.

"Let's go to the block party, okay?"
"You go. I'm in no mood for a party."
"You have to come. I was gonna ask you to dance with me."
This got her laughing.
"You and me, Anthony, what a sight that'll be!"
"Will ya?"
"What the hell, maybe it'll change my luck."

People dance in the street for this block party with exuberance I have never seen since. It was a unified happening of friends, neighbors, Josie, my mother and father, Rosie and Tommy, Theresa, Junior and Alfred, Grandpa, Gracie, and Uncles Andy, Willie, Aunt Anna and me. The veterans wear their army, navy, and marine uniforms one last time and everyone, including Theresa, dances jubilantly because we are dancing for the joy of those men who returned. We have no material wealth, no toys, no cars, televisions, or grand estates for the working class, yet, just proof that all is possible. We won the war. We have our answer: Freedom. We are No. 1 in the world. We dance for the truth of the moment, its happiness and camaraderie. We party with great equality, no age or class distinctions, just people who love America. The party ends in a conga line led by Aunt Anna and me. Near dawn, almost everyone has returned home. What remains is an empty, littered street and a blissful memory of American innocence, the end of World War II. An innocence that upon reflection was not so long ago, just long enough in time to be unknown to generations of Americans after mine.

CHAPTER 3

ANOTHER CLASS BELL is about to ring and as I check my watch I realize it's almost noon. It's time for lunch and the secretary might lock her office, so I leap down from the fourth-floor staircase and brush past a bull of a steel structured priest with the voice of a foghorn that scares me to death.

"Hey, Jack!"

Oh my God. It's Engles.

"What are you doing out of class?"

"I don't go to school here."

"Then what are you doing on the fourth floor?"

"Just looking around."

"Who said you could?"

"Fr. Ryan."

"You mean Mr. Ryan?"

"Yes, Mr. Ryan."

"Why?"

"I'm waiting to see Fr. Watson."

"He's not here today."

"Yes I know."

"So what are you waiting for if you know he's not here?"

"I'm waiting till he comes back."

"All day?"

"Yes."

"Why?"

"I want to talk to him."

"About what?"

"Well I'm waiting to talk to 'him.'"

"What do you want?"

"Well, I really want to talk to Fr. Watson."

"Go downstairs and wait. His office is on the first floor, not the fourth."

The bell rings and I descend the stairs, passing students who rush up the staircase but tone it down when they see Engles.

"Look out." "It's Freddie." "Watch it!"

I enter the headmaster's office breathless.

"Is he back?"

"You were gone a long time."

"Is he back?"

"No. Fr. Ryan said you met."

"He calls himself mister."

"He's practically a priest."

"He told me I could go upstairs."

"Did you?"

"Yes."

"And?"

"I learned a lot."

"You did?"

"Yes."

"Like what?"

"You know that priest who brought you the Greek grades this morning?"

"Fr. Culkin?"

"Yes. He spoke about life."

"What did he say?"

"It's a tight rope, but it all adds up."

"Sounds like Culkin."

"He's very tall."

"He was varsity basketball for Niagara before he became a Jesuit."

"I know people who don't know how to make it work."

"Life?"

"Yes, it's an easy thing to waste."

Nancy studies me for a second and realizes I have become pensive.

I sit.

I wait.

※

AFTER THE BLOCK PARTY, it was time to move. So, with no funds to speak of, my parents were forced to take an apartment on the furthest side of Brooklyn from my Aunt Anna and the Sbarra family. We moved to a three-bedroom apartment on the sixth and top floor of one of dozens of buildings known as the Fort Greene Projects, on Myrtle Avenue, near the Brooklyn navy yard in the neighborhood that later became known as the Blackboard Jungle. It was a neighborhood that was not innocent, warm and loving.

I was conflicted. Of course I wanted to see the world, finally, but it had never dawned on me that I had to leave the family I loved so much. With all those relatives around me daily, I had a culture from people who lived and breathed for each other. And now that they were exhausted from the war, I was abandoning them. I was to enter a world in turmoil due to neighbors in their own perpetual wars where they went to the street to get back what they lost or felt they deserved. These inhabitants suffered from lack of love and lack of family and dedicated their energy to destroying each other.

My mother proved she could make a good home for her family even under the worst of circumstances. My father would be his usual at-ease self. Theresa would grow into her teenage years with rage as her outlet, becoming a tomboy with fists to match her temper. And I would discover emotions by witnessing life in the raw.

We arrive the day after the paint job and the apartment has that awful smell. I have my own room, a new bed, and a new mattress, all of which alienate me because there are no traditions here. No warmth, no traces of Aunts Anna, Gracie, Dottie, Josie, or Grandma and Grandpa, and no sense of the past. I'm not alone in my isolation. To make matters worse, my mother and father are tense with each other. After an almost two-year war separation, they have to reinvest themselves. Theresa stops talking whenever anything upsets her, which is most of the time. Here we are, strangers to each other in a strange land surrounded with frustrated people for neighbors.

My mother is the most optimistic. With her furnishings returned from storage, she is forever attempting to find the best arrangements for her hand-carved sofa, armchairs, and tables, coffee table, bedroom set, and, of course, her kitchen continues to nurture all of us in the most happy of ways. "First things first" is my mother's theory, which means food. As we move into our apartment I stand in the midst of six-story brick buildings with no architectural character, covered in dirty snow. The residents are a conglomeration of races and nationalities of every culture, or lack thereof, bound by primal estrangement. Puerto Ricans. Hawaiians. Blacks. Asians. Whites.

The Fort Greene Projects are reality personified! They are intimidating, cold, pre-war, gold and red brick buildings, spare and practical. Romance, of every kind, belongs somewhere else. As I scan the environment, I realize that in my mother's anxiety to reconstruct her home she forgot to notice the figures in the view. Though her motto was "Where there's a will, there's a way," I wonder how well she'll be able to fulfill her motto here.

Boxes are everywhere. Uncle Andy enters, breathless, carrying a sofa with Uncle Alfred and my father.

"My purple heart is turning black."

"Let's send the bastard back so they can finish the job," Uncle Alfred tells my father.

My mother enters from the kitchen.

"Put the sofa against that wall."

My father asks Uncle Alfred.

"How come we didn't get shot?"

Then he tells Uncle Andy.

"You must have walked in front of a bullet just to get a furlough."

"You guys didn't get shot cause you spent all your time dealing on the black market."

My father argues.

"Who you kidding? I saw more action than any of you."

After getting her sofa where she wants it, my mother starts back to the kitchen when Theresa enters with boxes.

"What are these?"

"Dishes."

She helps Theresa to the kitchen. My father tells the others.

"Let's get the beds."

BROOKLYN ODYSSEY 75

Breathless Uncle Andy feigns.

"What the enemy couldn't do to me?"

Aunt Dottie is preparing dinner when Theresa and my mother enter the kitchen. My mother wants to know.

"Where's your brother?"

"In the clouds, where he always is!"

Of course I'm lurking nearby the entire time. As my mother exits the kitchen she tells Theresa.

"Get him to help."

Theresa sees me and shouts back.

"He's not my son. You like him. You get him."

My mother tries to pick up a heavy box and sees me.

"Anthony, give me a hand."

We take it to my new bedroom and I ask.

"Have you seen the people around here?"

She busies herself with boxes.

"I mind my own business. You do the same."

"What do you mean?"

"Stay out of trouble."

"What trouble?"

"Any trouble. You hear me?"

"Like what?"

"You think the world is so wonderful. You're old enough now. Go take a look! But if you can't handle yourself out there, stay home. And don't ever get your father to fight somebody for you or I'll kill you myself. If something happens you have to talk about, tell me, you hear?"

"I don't know what you're talking about."

"I think you do."

"If this is such a bad neighborhood, why did we move here?"

"There are good people anywhere and bad people. Learn to pick and choose. If you see something bad, keep moving. Monday I'm starting a job and you're beginning school. So mark my words: *"Tu parle quanda piesca aline!"*

"What?"

"Tu parle quanda piesca aline!"

"Thanks, Mom! I meant what does it mean?"

"It means you talk when the chicken pees."

I laugh because she could always make me laugh. She starts to leave the bedroom. I really want to know.

"What does that mean?"

"Since the chicken never pees, it means keep your mouth shut."

I follow her into the living room.

"The chicken never pees? How do you know that?"

"Anthony, have you ever seen a chicken pee?"

This time I laugh hysterically. She's thrilled with herself.

"Right? You have no answer this time, huh?"

My father and uncles are drinking beer in the kitchen when we walk in.

Aunt Dottie wants to know.

"How soon you want to eat?"

My father answers.

"Dottie, whenever you're ready."

"In about ten minutes."

I take the opportunity to make my announcement.

"Momma says chickens never pee."

Uncle Andy, always the clown, acts this out, "I wish you hadn't told me that. I'll never be able to eat another chicken, thinking all his urine is inside."

Dottie assures him.

"I'm broiling steaks with baked potatoes and spinach, so you don't have to worry for tonight."

But this doesn't stop Uncle Andy.

"How long do chickens live? Think about it, Anthony, no peeing your whole life. What pains you would have."

He acts out a chicken stuffed with urine. We all laugh, as Theresa enters, quizzical about the joke she is left out of. Then Andy asks my mother.

"Helen, where did you ever get such an idea?"

"*Tu parle quanda piesca aline* Alfred, you Remember."

Uncle Alfred remembers.

"Momma's favorite expression."

BROOKLYN ODYSSEY

Then he tells Dottie and Andy, the two youngest of the aunts and uncles.

"You two weren't born yet."

Aunt Dottie teases.

"Our family legacy built on chickens that never pee. No wonder we have to spend our lives washing and ironing."

I chime in.

"I'll change all that."

I sing. "Give me five minutes more, only five minutes more."

As I sing I start to dance, moving to embrace Theresa.

"Let me stay in your arms evermore."

She pushes me backward.

"Get outta here, creep."

Aunt Dottie teases me.

"What a voice. Anthony, become an accountant. You're good at arithmetic."

"If I dance in movies, you wouldn't have to wash and iron anymore."

Dottie changes her mind.

"Suddenly your voice sounds better. I like this kid."

Then she and I jitterbug together, singing,

"All week long I dream about our Saturday date."

And thus we become residents of the Fort Greene Projects.

※

MY PARENTS WERE CONCERNED about Theresa living in this neighborhood. They assumed she was vulnerable because she was a girl, which only made Theresa more aggressive to prove herself. I was a boy, and in an Italian American household, boys wind up with the best of all possible worlds. As a boy you are spoiled rotten, babied and loved within the home, and treated like a prince who has no household chores, especially if you like school, as I did. Then, when you enter the world, at seven or so, they assume you can take care of yourself, or at least that you should learn to take care of yourself.

My mother was precise. "If you ever get into trouble and cause your father to go out and fight for you, I'll kill you. Solve your own problems, or don't go out."

Short and sweet! I chose to go out and solve my own problems.

Theresa is stronger than most of the neighborhood, so she starts to prove herself by punching it out with boys older than herself. One of them usually winds up with a bloody nose. I, on the other hand, have a mouth thanks to a family who allowed me to be outspoken, and that becomes my power. I could talk my way out of strange entanglements.

A Puerto Rican kid named August, two years my senior, makes and sells guns, and wants to sell me one. I realize immediately that this is not data to share with the family. If I want to retain my freedom in the world, there are aspects of street reality witnessed, but not admitted. The strongest tradition in our household is from an old family custom, based on a very simple process of peasant thought. Any request involving food and the home, the answer is always "yes." Any request involving chances and expanding in the world, the answer is always "no."

I decide to take dance classes. My father is annoyed that I haven't grown out of this phase during the war and keeps asking me why I want to dance. How do you explain such a thing, especially at eight or nine years old?

"I like it."

But somehow that is always the wrong thing to say. My family is attempting to patch up our lives. My mother takes a job, which upsets my father's ego. My father works for the City Sanitation Department and studies nights to advance himself through a series of tests, and I want to dance. And to dance in the midst of a neighborhood where people are shooting each other. Go figure! But I want to dance. I love trying to choreograph spontaneously to music. I love the frenzy involved in crescendos and the dizzying feelings from the movements. So my father offers.

"Well, I'll look around for a place for you to take dance classes."

How funny! On Myrtle Avenue nothing exists but brute reality, yet I expect my father to find a dance school. I accompany my dances with inventions of my own humming. This is the period I discover Gene Kelly and more of Fred Astaire. They bring so much pleasure to their work. I want to create one big jamboree for my angry neighbors.

I notice, however, other kids are not dancing in this environment. They are exploring savage natures instead. I follow a gang of kids rushing down the back staircase. The two boxers are one black boy against two Puerto Ricans, almost teenagers. They are fighting brutally, egged on by bystanders who jeer "goddamn spics" "fucking nigger" to make them fight harder. Clearly the mob wants blood. I become disturbed by their brutality and rush off. I feel like such an opposite. I want to entertain people by singing or dancing. My neighbors want to break noses, kick each other's balls, bite ears, and cause bruises and wounds. To make matters worse, I have to be careful in what I reveal at home, for being a shut-in again would be worse.

So now I inhabit three worlds. Home, where my parents provide the basics brilliantly; school, where the nuns teach reading, writing, and arithmetic, which I perfected long before I ever went to school so I am automatically the class champ; and the jungle of the projects, which provide life, bad as it is. I conquer each of the three. At home I know how to manipulate my family, except for Theresa, and I'm basically free to come and go. At school, nuns like a student who reads and writes and enjoys going to the blackboard to parse complex-compound sentences. Of the three worlds, I am most attracted to the jungle because at home my family is in denial. They're huddled together in their wonderful nest but not open to this world and its problems. They discover television. Between their nine-to-five jobs, their love of their home, and their evenings at the tube, they're devoted to having found only one answer, contentment, and dreaming of moving to a better neighborhood. There is nothing they need here in the projects. And nothing about the projects causes them to seek answers to any questions, since they ask none. The same with the nuns who already have the answers they consider important to a good catholic boy, memorized from the Baltimore catechism, so they too ask no questions.

The jungle within these projects is disgusting, offensive, and frightening but full of questions. Animosity thy name is neighbors! They hate each other. And they are so diverse in their lack of cultures that they represent the entire globe. This makes me feel I travel the universe daily. My mother admonishes me.

"If you look for trouble, you'll find it. Turn around and you will see something better. The world is just as good as it is bad."

But I couldn't look the other way. Trouble was like a magnet to me.

I throw up from what I see, get cold sweats from things that intimidate me. But I look. I cannot be sociologically blind. The projects are my UN. And I begin to see how equally divided the world is between good and evil. Fifty/fifty became my measuring cup. Fifty percent of these nationalities are good people like my family trying to have productive lives, and fifty percent are not. And the fifty/fifty came from each nationality. This was a distinction I would carry throughout my life, that no one group holds all the good or all the bad. What began to happen to me has lasted throughout my life. Odd as it may seem, I began to dislike answers, quick ones in any case. My family did have answers after all, but their answers were simplistic. The nuns did have answers, but these were easy conclusions.

The projects cause me to seek questions, complicated ones. Compound issues that make simple answers inadequate. In school I find myself frustrated by true-or-false exams, or even multiple choice, because I find fault with the simplicity of each side as an answer. I like essays. I become the most successful pupil to parse compound-complex sentences because, in most cases, such sentences are complicated enough to avoid clichés or pat answers and force me to think outside the box, to search for truth.

Life begins to come alive to me the more I witness its complications. Evil frightens, but why hide from it? Troubles surround me. Residents aim to kill each other. Races band together in petty wars without much rhyme or reason. Why? What good is any of this? How will this benefit not just our society but even these very people themselves? Where is God? What is God? How do we measure up to His plan for us? Who are the atheists and how did they find no God when they witness the birth of babies, or watch birds fly through clouds against a blue sky? How come God is so real to me? Have I simply made Him up, or been brainwashed, or do I really relate to Him and feel His presence as I claim?

My mother admonishes me to imitate Brent, a black boy who lives in the apartment directly below ours and who was born the same day and year I was born. She enumerates.

"Brent does everything right. He runs track in the morning with his father. He comes straight home after school every day to babysit his little sister, goes to the stores, helps to cook."

And, according to my mother, if one could believe her, "Irons clothes for his mother."

Brent is living in the projects until he can move out. In the meantime he is hiding. Brent is not mixing, not experiencing life in the projects. No wonder my mother admires him. And, of course, the projects are no place to study dancing. Even I finally figure this out. I never can make anyone in the family see the seriousness of my desire anyway. They successfully make me feel that I am not talented, so why bother. Ending my song-and-dance career is strike one against me. I do not have enough fight to win this one, nor the talent.

❋

IT'S TWENTY MINUTES past noon and the secretary wonders.

"Getting tired?"

"No. I'm fine."

"It's lunchtime. I'll have to close the office for an hour."

I immediately rise nervously.

"That's okay. I'll wait in the hallway."

"You can get a sandwich around the corner. Follow the seniors. They're allowed out at lunchtime."

"What if he comes back?"

"Then he'll be in the office."

"You sure?"

"I'm sure."

"Okay."

I stand up. She asks.

"Where do you live?"

"Kings Highway and Coney Island Avenue."

"Pretty far away. How did you get here?"

"The BMT to Prospect Avenue, then the Franklin Avenue line for one stop."

"You obviously know your way around."

"Well, I've lived all over Brooklyn."

"How come?"

"During the war we lived on Avenue U with my grandparents and my aunts. After the war we moved to the Fort Greene Projects near the navy yard. Last year we moved back to the same apartment we lived in before the war, on Coney Island Avenue. You get to know Brooklyn."

"Sounds like a lifetime to me. I've lived in the same house since I was born."

"Well, the war, you know!"

"With all those aunts and grandparents, I'll bet they spoiled you."

"If you can't be born a prince, be the son in an Italian family."

I like making her laugh.

"Do you have money for lunch?"

"Yes, thank you."

I'm touched by her concern.

"I have five dollars my Aunt Anna gave me for my birthday."

"When was that?"

"Yesterday."

"How old are you?"

"Fourteen."

"Happy Birthday!"

"Thank you."

When I turn to leave her office, she calls after me.

"Anthony, your jacket!"

"I don't need it."

"It's cold."

"That's okay!"

"I won't forget. I promise."

I smile at her, then take my coat and exit. It's clear she likes me, despite my intruding upon her privacy. The school bell rings, seniors rush to their lockers and leave the building for lunch. I'm glad Nancy has insisted I take my jacket, for I've forgotten the street has mounds of dirty snow and it is cold. I follow a group as Mr. Carney cynically imitates his teacher.

"Mr. Carney, you're gonna get kicked out!"

A second senior demonstrates concern.

"Twelve seniors were booted last month, so don't think you're safe."

Mr. Carney defends himself.

"I'm trying."

A third senior adds.

"Fr. Hill helped me learn trigonometry last year. Go to him."

Many of the seniors smoke cigarettes openly as they walk away from the school. I admire their poise and their power as young men, hoping some day to be one of them, but find it intimidating. I follow them to their restaurant.

✳

NOW THAT TELEVISIONS were for sale and because we were World War II winners, we were number one in our own eyes and free to do and have whatever might satisfy even prurient interest. By the winter of 1948, manufacturers could sell you all the things you needed to be happy. By this time I was witnessing life in the projects none of the manufacturers were even trying to produce cures.

On the Christmas of 1949, an enormous, empty box invades our living room. Our ugly black-and-white television now sits next to our decorated Christmas tree, too incongruous for sore eyes. That night my parents are putting on their coats after dinner. Theresa is watching roller derby. I return home. My mother tells me.

"Dinner's on the stove. Where were you?"

"The movies. Where you going?"

"Aunt Anna is sick."

"What's the matter?"

"Her nerves got the best of her."

"What do you mean?"

"We'll tell you tomorrow when we know."

"I want to know now."

"We don't know ourselves."

"I'm going with you."

"It's no place for you."

"Tell me what happened."

"The War! Grandma's death! Aunt Anna was never herself again."

My father adds so I can have the basics.

"She's in a hospital."

"Why?"

My mother gets teary-eyed. "The doctors want to look at her for awhile, so they can see what's wrong. There's shrimp and flounder on the stove, a sweet potato and broccoli in the dish. Do your homework and get to bed early."

"We'll be back late so don't worry."

My father and mother exit. Theresa speaks to the back of my head.

"She had a nervous breakdown. The doctors are going to give her shock treatments. They thought it would upset you to know."

I can barely move, but I manage to turn to Theresa.

"How could this happen?"

"It happened."

I run to my room. What to do? My family never prepared for these things. Aunt Anna is going to need something they cannot give her. What are shock treatments? I often wonder if commitment to become an activist began for me in that moment.

At three a.m. I am sitting at my window, shivering. I am positive that there has to be an answer to this situation. At five thirty a.m. I go to Sacred Heart Church across the street from the navy yard. The congregation is several elderly people and me. When I go to communion, I am ice cold from the early morning walk, the cold church, and my nerves. I don't believe I prayed. I think I just felt awful and assumed God would figure it out. What I suspect is that that day I created the next covenant between God and me. If He would cure my godmother, I would cure His world. After all, I ended WWII with a makeshift altar hidden in a bedroom. Now I am in his church. How hard could this be?

Mass is over around 6:00 a.m., and when I leave the church, I walk right into a fight spilling out onto the stoop of a tenement. A black man is fighting a Puerto Rican, egged on by family and neighbors everywhere, all in their underwear. "*Maricón.*" "Goddam spics." "*Pajaro.*" Police cars arrive and I walk away, made despondent by the violence and knowing it is ridiculously unimportant. After all, Aunt Anna is sick. What else matters? When I return to our apartment my parents are dressed for work and drinking coffee. As soon as I open the door, I hear my name.

"Anthony?"

It's my father.

"Yeah."

"Where were you?"
I enter the kitchen.
"Church."
"Breakfast?"
"No."
My father leaves for work.
"I'll boil two eggs," Mom suggests.
"I don't want them. What did the doctor say?"
"It'll take awhile."
"What's wrong with her?"
"She needs to get her health back again."
"What happened to her?"
"Life, what else?"
"What will make her well again?"
With tears she says.
 "I don't know."
"Does anybody know?"
"On Sunday we'll bring samples of food to remind her."
"Of what?"
"Of her cooking. Maybe that'll bring her back?"
"You mean she doesn't remember? You gotta bring her food to remind her who she is?"
"She's very sick."
"Is she gonna get well?"
"What am I a psychiatrist? How the hell do I know?"
I lose it.
"Does anybody in our family ever know anything?"
I storm off.

*

ON NOSTRAND AVENUE I watch the seniors from outside the ice cream parlor, for I'm too intimidated to follow them in. Then I cross to a candy store and buy two frankfurters. As I stand and watch them from across the street, I wonder what they know of life's tragedies. Is it possible that I have more knowledge of life, thanks to the realities I experienced in the projects. Do these guys have friends from different races?

Did they enter Prep with certain barriers and prejudices, and overcome them at Brooklyn Prep, as promised in class this morning?

※

My best friend, Carl Cruikshank, lives in the project building across from ours, so we explore Brooklyn and Manhattan as if we're Tom Sawyer and Huck Finn. Carl is older than me and heavyset by nature. He has beautiful blue/black skin and his parents say they're grateful I'm his friend so I can protect him. Odd, that they see a scrawny white boy as Carl's protector, only because I am so outspoken they think I can take care of Carl. In fact, they're right. I move about the projects with great confidence that no one is going to hurt us, and whenever someone tries, I speak so confidently they believe I can take them in a major fight, when deep down I know I can't even beat up Theresa. Carl, on the other hand, laughs off every threat against us. It's his good nature to see trouble as too difficult to conquer so he just laughs.

Carl and I explore Myrtle Avenue with its overhead rickety rusty El train that creaks from half a mile away whenever any train is coming. Beneath it are mysteries as, for instance, when a man walks over to us and asks us to do him a favor. We are to bring a small box to one of the Project buildings approximately three blocks away to the second floor apartment and just give it to the person who opens the door. He gives us his pocket full of change, which is approximately three dollars. When we arrive at that building, we know instantly this is the building of a recent murder. By the time we climb to the apartment on the second floor, we're convinced this was the very apartment of the murder. We knock with caution, and when the door opens we pass the box to a person who closes the door without thanking us.

We run home to our courtyard, where both of our buildings face each other and where we find my father doing what he most always does as he returns from work, having a baseball catch with teenage boys and Theresa. My father is a great athlete and the teenagers love to throw with him. You can hear the sound of that hardball as it enters each of their gloves and resounds throughout the courtyard of these ugly brick buildings. Carl and I are running fast for fear the cops might be following us or even the murderer. I yell over my shoulder as we part.

"Six o'clock!"

"Okay."

I run into my building and then into the closing doors of the elevator to find myself alone with crazy Murray, eighteen years old, mentally challenged, weighted down with rusty pots, a rusty washing board, a rusty iron, and two long rusty pipes. Murray works at some job but spends his earnings buying rusty junk. As long as it's rusty, he buys it until all his week's earnings are used up, and then he goes home and his orthodox Jewish parents scream and holler at him for hours. They live on the sixth floor as we do.

"Anthony? Do me a favor."

"What?"

"If my parents are home, would you hold my things for me?"

"Where?"

"In your place."

Speaking sarcastically, "That would make my mother real happy."

But my words fall on deaf ears.

"Thanks."

"Murray, don't you understand anything?"

This goes right over his head. When we reach the sixth floor, Murray exits first, surreptitiously, and whispers to me.

"Knock on my door. See if anyone is home?"

"What if they are? What do I say?"

"Nothing. Just see if they're there."

"Murray, if they open the door, I have to say something."

"Just walk away."

"I'll tell them that you want to come home. Okay?"

"Good. That'll be good."

I turn the corner down the other hallway and knock on their door. When there's no answer I call to Murray.

"They're not home."

Murray comes around the corner.

"Do you have a key?"

"Yes."

I watch Murray enter his apartment with all his rusty junk.

Later that night, in our kitchen, Carl is a guest for dinner. We're halfway through the meal of southern fried chicken, mashed potatoes, carrots, spinach, and a pan of eggplant parmigiana, and my mother is trying to calm Theresa down.

"They're supposed to take care of themselves. They're boys."

"I can fight better than he can."

And she can. But she lacks my skill at making everyone believe I'll win if we start the fight. The only one who knows that I'm full of shit is Theresa.

"What kind of talk is that for a girl?"

My mother wants to know. My father tries, as usual, a safer topic. So he asks Carl.

"Do you play baseball?"

"Yeah."

"Why don't the two of you form a team?"

Mom asks. "Carl, you like the eggplant?"

But before he can answer heavy yelling can be heard around the hallway. Theresa leaps up, sensing fun. She yells back. "It's Murray."

I join her and we head for the door, but Mom blocks us.

"Get back. You don't go and watch people's suffering. That poor family has enough trouble without you two adding to it."

Murray and his father are screaming, and Murray's mother is crying hysterically. His father yells. My mother starts to get us back to the table to finish dinner under the angers of Murray and his father.

"Don't come back! We don't want you here!"

Murray yells at his father.

"Fuck you!."

"Go, and don't ever come back."

"I hate you both."

My mother tells us, "They don't need you to add to their grief. That embarrasses them. You have no manners? They're orthodox people. God has given them some cross with Murray."

At that moment Murray's mother screams.

"My eyes! Ouch!"

My mother is up instantly, "Oh my God!" She quickly grabs a kitchen towel, wets it, and rushing to the hallway, followed by my father. Theresa, Carl, and I are close behind. My mother rushes to Murray's mother, who is on her knees bleeding. Murray must have hit her with one of his rusty irons. My father places himself between Murray and his father. Theresa, Carl, and I watch from a distance. Murray's father is yelling.

"Stay away from us! Don't ever come back! We don't want you here!"

Furious, Murray knows the best way to hurt them. He begins yelling at the top of his lungs for the whole world to hear.

"Guns for the Arabs, shit for the Jews!"

This causes his parents excruciating pain. A knife in their bellies could not have been worse. Murray runs to the staircase.

"Guns for the Arabs, shit for the Jews!"

His father rushes into the apartment, returns with a handful of dishes, and throws them at Murray from the top of the stairs. Murray is proclaiming the first ever intifada down the staircase.

"Guns for the Arabs, shit for the Jews!"

His mother is doubled over in tears. She has a cut on her forehead that's bleeding profusely while my mother is washing it. His father runs into his apartment for more dishes, which he flings, hitting Murray occasionally as Murray's voice echoes and resounds throughout the building's staircase.

"Gunns foorr tthhee Arraabbss, SSSHHIITT fffoorrrr tthheee JJJJJJJJEeeeeeewwwwssss!!!" Murray's mother runs into her apartment, taking my mother's wet towel with her. Murray's father follows her in. Carl says.

"I better go home.

My mother is never without a finish to her meal.

"Not yet. I made apple pie."

Carl and I witnessed chains and brass knuckles as every Saturday night dance of death in the Fort Greene Park across Myrtle Avenue when teenagers were determined to destroy each other. They returned the next day with the scars of war all across their faces, arms, and legs. The softness of my grandfather and his unconditional love never existed in this place. These contrasts provided my future sense for irony. First, I was having a good time being a kid in Sacred Heart grammar school, enjoying reading, writing, and arithmetic despite the crazy world surrounding me; and, second, my obligation to cure my Aunt Anna gave me a power to connect to God. It also forced me to wake up every morning and go to Mass and communion. The covenant I created with God had to work. After all, when Aunt Anna told me to end the war, I did. So how hard could it be to cure Aunt Anna? Not a bad combination, to have a secure home life, an education for the basics, a love of God, and to witness a world of evils abounding. The projects provided me with huge experiences. Throughout a career in theatre, where I directed diverse plays in separate styles and a variety of peoples, I often felt my ease of working with these plays resulted from the four years I roamed the Fort Greene Projects.

※

WHILE AUNT ANNA SUFFERS the indignity of a mental hospital, my family thinks they have the best solution to cure her. Because she is such a tremendous cook, they bring her samples every Sunday of all the foods she usually makes. Their theory is simple. They want Aunt Anna to taste this food as if she cooked it, to remind her of her life at home. Fortunately, I have a covenant with God to make it all work out, so I let the family believe whatever they want to believe.

On this Sunday morning my mother and father, Aunts Josie and Gracie, Grandpa and Uncle Willie enter our kitchen. They are returning from church. My mother tells her sisters.

"I have to heat up the minestrone."

But she and Aunt Josie overlap this week, so Aunt Josie explains, "I brought minestrone."

My mother is the only person I ever met who had a true sense of complete sharing. Whatever was needed by anyone was her favorite thing to do. She seemed to live without personal needs, other than her home, our family, all the relatives, and good neighbors.

Aunt Gracie is forever giving food away so extra minestrone is fine with her. "That's all right, the other patients will eat it."

Josie tells my mother, "Dottie's bringing butter cookies that Anna taught her to make."

My father reminds them. "It takes an hour by car. The trains double the time. So we better get going."

I enter the kitchen and Aunt Gracie asks me.

"Anthony, do you ever miss Mass?"

My mother shows how proud she is. "We can't keep him home even when he has a fever. Nine months, every day!"

I take my chance.

"Can I go with you today?"

"For the fiftieth time, no. You're too young. We tell you that every week."

"I'll wait outside."

"You don't want to see all that. It's a mental hospital."

"I don't care. I want to see her."

Mom tells me.

"Aunt Anna is getting better. Last week her spirits were good, and she knew who we were."

Uncle Willie says.

"We gotta go. I told Tommy and Rosie we would be there by twelve thirty."

As Willie, my mother, Josie, Gracie, and Grandpa exit, my father suggests, "Finish your homework. Remember we'll do everything to support your education. But you have to hold your own with your grades. We can't do that for you."

"I want to go with you."

"You're too young. They won't let you in."

"I'll wait in the car. She can come to the window. At least I could see her. I'll bring the homework. Come on, Dad!"

"Okay, let's try it."

We arrive in early afternoon. I remain in the car, alone, my eyes riveted on a window at the Kings County Mental Ward. She does not come to the window. But we do this every week and I sit in that car for months of Sundays, waiting in the heat, in the cold. On one of those Sundays, the windows are covered with snow, so I turn on the ignition and use the windshield wipers. The frustration of waiting makes me so much older that my argyle sweater begins to fit.

As I wait, I imagine Aunt Anna's childhood when at ten years old they encased her in a full body cast over her head. Then at twelve they take the cast off and discover that her spine grew into a hump, so they try to stretch her. I also recall the panic on Aunt Anna's stunned face in the funeral parlor when Grandma died. As I imagine these scenes, I listen to beautiful music on the car radio. I hear the Tchaikovsky Piano Concerto #1 for the first time in my life. What a thrill! I fantasize how this music could tame all the suffering in the projects. In the world!

❊

I FINISH MY FRANKFURTERS, knish, and soda before the seniors leave their restaurant. I walk back to Prep, but lunch hour is not over yet. So I sit on the stoop of a brownstone across from the school. I wonder how many of these preppies were pampered in summer camps or travels abroad? I assume they have all the things I've always wanted, but that means they don't have the projects. How many even know the world of the Fort Greene Projects? I pray for the suffering families like Murray's. Are these preppies even aware of such a family?

It's too cold, so I go inside the brownstone doorway to crouch against a wall, shivering. The fire in my belly is losing its flame! I'm beginning to lose resolve. Watching the maturity of the seniors begins to weaken my belief in myself, to make me think that I don't have what it takes to win this battle. The projects provided many questions that need resolutions, but what if I never find the answers? I will then have a stomach filled with human pain and suffering but no tools to ease them.

This causes me to compare the easy lives of these preppies with those who suffer in the projects, for instance. I recall a snowy afternoon in 1950 when I returned home from Sacred Heart with an armful of books. I hear angry shouting as I approach an excited mob. I witness two women ripping each other's clothes off. The Hawaiian is practically bare-chested. The Puerto Rican is bleeding from the nose. Bloodthirsty neighbors are egging them on. The Puerto Rican shouts.

"*Hija de puta!*"

The Hawaiian shouts.

"If you give your husband what he needs he wouldn't come to me, bitch!"

"*El coño de tu madre gonorrea!*"

This delights the crowd who are shouting obscenities, overlapping the fighters.

"Don't take that shit from that spic!"

"*Rómpele la cabeza!*"

"Rip her tits off, she'll have nothing to give him!"

A hand grabs me by my neck. It's my mother, returning home from work. She pushes me toward our building.

"Don't contribute to their madness by watching crazy women. They have nothing better to do all day than act worse than men. What the hell are you doing there?"

"Everybody hates each other. What a world!"

"Half of the world gets along. You look in all the wrong directions, Anthony. I keep telling you to turn around, you'll see something good."

My mother goes to the mailboxes. I press the button for the elevator.

"Can we get a piano?"

"This something new?"

"I want a piano."

"Why do you want a piano?"

"I want one."

"Do you know how to play the piano?"

"How could I know how to play the piano, Mom?"

"Well if you don't know how to play the piano, what do you want a piano for?"

Of course she makes me laugh. Her illogic always does since I know she intends to be funny but intends at the same time to get out of really dealing with such a request. So I follow her into the elevator.

"I could learn, take lessons."

"Every five minutes you put in for a bid. If it's not one thing it's another. When you see me coming, I think you make up things just to aggravate me."

"I like music."

"Turn on the radio. That's why we have it."

"I want to learn how to play it."

"What family do you think you were born into, the Rockefellers? It's gonna take us ten more years to catch up from that war. We have no money for a piano, or lessons, and no room for it in any case. Stick to your schoolwork. You'll go further. We're just starting to get back on our feet."

We're still "arguing" as we enter the kitchen where Theresa is cooking.

"I wanted to dance. You wouldn't let me. Now I want to play the piano. You won't let me."

Theresa takes her usual chance to insult me.

"You gotta be kidding. Piano?"

My mother defends herself.

"You've been jumping around since you could walk. You wanna dance, dance. It's good exercise. I never stopped you."

"You know what I'm talking about."

Theresa drowns out our argument by singing at the top of her lungs. "Tura lura lura, tura lura laaaaaaaaaaa!!!!!!!!!!!!!!!"

We're stunned by her rage, the worse, and we don't know how to deal with it.

※

ONE AFTERNOON I hear shouts coming below our sixth story projects' staircase and discover Theresa boxing with a boy her age. I did not know how to deal with this, so I quietly slip into my bedroom, sit at my desk, and imagine playing the piano, using all ten fingers on a non-existent keyboard. I try to hear the Tchaikovsky concerto in my head. Later that evening, while I'm doing homework, I'm distracted by the noisy television so I go into the living room and see my mother, father, and Theresa enjoying the idiot humor of Milton Berle talking to his live audience. . . .

"My mother's in the first row. (to his mother) Hi Mom! (to the audience) She came by to pick up my paycheck."

My family laughs with the audience as a commercial for a Lucky Strike cigarette and match box dance.

"Turn that down. I can't study."

Theresa shouts.

"It's over in ten minutes."

"I have a history test tomorrow."

But even my father, who I could most often depend on for sanity, calls to me.

"Come and watch. Then you can study."

I go into the living room. My mother tries to lure me with food.

"There's ice cream in the freezer."

"I hate ice cream. You know that."

Theresa is always out for a fight.

"Where the hell did you get him from?"

"When any of you find out, send me back."

Milton Berle returns to the screen, dressed as a woman.

"Mom, I've been meaning to tell you something."

Again, his audience and my family laugh.

"Your kitchen's on fire!"

Berle sings, "There once was a sailor from France Who decided to take off his pants. Wait! Momma you can't leave yet. Come back! Momma! You forgot to pay the check!"

There are uproars of audience laughter shared in my living room. I lose it.

"And we can't afford a piano?"

Then I storm off to study, aware that my family is hiding from the basic life surrounding us right at our projects doorsteps. They see. They know of it even, but they are not going to become involved in anything other than their personal security. Hear no evil. See no evil. Television!

❃

FROM INSIDE the brownstone hallway, I see seniors returning so I follow them back into Prep. Instantly, I experience that roar and energy of students rushing to classes, only this time I'm overwhelmed by it. Clearly the waiting is discouraging me and I am feeling inadequate. Once again, the bell rings and, as if by magic, they evaporate. I am in total silence. I rush to the headmaster's office and find Nancy unlocking the door on her return from lunch. She anticipates me.

"Not yet."

I follow her in. Then I sit with my coat on, shivering. She wants to know.

"You all right?"

"I got cold."

She starts her work but keeps an eye on me.

I wait.

※

THE FORT GREEN PROJECTS are on Myrtle Avenue, and across Myrtle Avenue is Fort Greene Park, where teenagers gather in the evenings to beat each other up. Carl and I watch from behind trees and smoke Camels. Carl has such a good heart. He stares at this madness the way people might stare at lions fighting tigers. Clearly Carl has not one ounce of evil within himself, so violence makes him laugh, because, I guess, to him violence has no value, just pure insanity.

August, a twelve-year old Puerto Rican, sneaks up behind us to sell us a gun.

"Have you decided yet?"

He asks this of Carl, who never knows how to say no to such a silly question.

"I forgot about it."

August insults Carl.

"You dumb nigger. You wouldn't even know how to use this gun."

August and I have been through this scene before.

"Have you made up your mind?"

"You make them yourself?"

"Anthony, you ask me that every time. You want it or not?"

"Bullets too?"

"Bullets are extra. You know that."

To outfox the fox, "I'll have to save up."

"You keep saying the same fucking thing. Yes or no?"

"Of course I want it. I'll ask my mother for the money."

"I know you're not that stupid. Don't pull my dick. If you don't want it, then say no."

"Why don't you let me have it and I'll pay you when I get the money."

"Bullshit. Get the money, you get the gun! Keep your mouth shut about this, you hear me? I could get in a lot of trouble."

"Of course. We know that."

August runs off on an open field. I whisper to Carl.

"Watch this."

Then I shout loud enough for any police station within two miles radius.

"August . . . !"

He turns.

"What?"

"I'll give you a quarter each week until I pay it up."

"Get the money first. All of it."

"That'll take me too long."

"I'm not giving this to you for nothing, so forget it."

August starts off. I feign anger.

"Thanks a lot."

Over his shoulder to me as he starts off again, he shouts.

"Fuck you!"

To Carl, I whisper again.

"I know how to break his balls."

Then, as loud as I can, I call.

"August, sell me that gun. I really want it."

His body jerks to a stop as he quickly spins around three hundred and sixty degrees to see if any police heard me.

"Shut up, you crazy, fucking bastard!"

We stare each other down. Then August runs off. Carl and I have a good laugh. Though we are still innocent Carl and I are becoming streetwise. On hot summer days Carl and I roam Myrtle Avenue, Fort Greene Park, and the navy yard in search of adventure and find the Brooklyn Bridge. We leave early mornings on the pretense that we'll be playing in the park all day, but we walk to the bridge and cross it. In fact we never have to make excuses, since no one ever needs to know what we're doing on hot summer days. Like Tom and Huck, we explore the cave, only in this case it's the maze of lower Manhattan and as much of Brooklyn as we can explore before nightfall. On one occasion we discover aquarium shops with tropical fish around Canal Street and this becomes one of our favorite haunts. I save up and return to purchase a tank, gravel, a snail, and two guppies. I fight with my mother, who tries to prevent me from entering our apartment with my aquarium. She insultingly refers to it.

"The mess only an idiot would bring into a house."

And Theresa is right, as usual.

"You let him do whatever he wants, so why don't you admit it, and stop all this bullshit?"

"Watch your tongue."

My mother becomes sidetracked with Theresa as I slide past with my "mess." The guppies stay. And multiply. Within a few weeks there are hundreds of these ugly little things. I watch them fall out of their mother's like crumbs dropping from Gretel's pockets. The smell from the tank is not likely to ingratiate my mother.

"Clean the tank, or throw the whole thing away."

"I don't have to clean it. The snail does that."

"Idiot, can't you smell a cesspool? The nuns think you are so smart. I should bring them home and let them get to know you."

"I'll get a filter."

And I do. But nothing can combat these fertile little breeders.

So, one Saturday my mother decides to clean the tank while I'm out, of course. She has successfully thrown away my WWII booty, and dismantled my altar, so she obviously feels she can get away with anything she wants. But a tank filled with water is heavy. She barely carries it into the kitchen and has to lift it to place it in the sink. In doing this, she shatters the glass against the enamel side of the sink and is attacked by six hundred nervous guppies diving into whatever ounce of water they can find spreading across her impeccably waxed kitchen floor and under her refrigerator and stove. It takes her all day and night to clean up gravel, broken glass and dead fish. I play out this tragedy for all it's worth. I insist she broke her promise to keep her hands off the tank.

She insists, "I promised no such thing."

Somehow I make her feel guilty enough to pay to replace all of it.

"All right, but get a better tank and the right filter. Make sure you know what you are doing this time."

Theresa is fit to be tied. So I outfit a larger tank filled with beautiful mollies and angelfish, and learn that something good can come from almost anything. Theresa is so angry she becomes speechless rather than waste her breath on any more of my idiocy.

Carl and I discover the Peerless movie house on Myrtle Avenue.

It becomes our home every Saturday afternoon. For twelve cents they show feature films (at least two), newsreels, comic strips, and a serial like the Perils of Pauline. Underneath the screen is the candy counter, where people purchase peanut chews, ice cream, and popcorn during the movie. Then the owner goes up and down the aisles yelling, "Peanuts, popcorn, ice cream," making quiet aesthetic appreciation almost impossible, but, of course all noise is welcomed with the kind of movies we are seeing.

Carl and I, and several other friends, develop an evil trick so that only one of us has to pay and we can use our twelve cents to buy candy. The lobby is always mobbed when we arrive to buy tickets, because they don't begin to sell the tickets until a short time before the movie. So we scatter through the crowd and begin to cause commotions, sometimes with sounds, other times by pushing each other into other people as if we are fighting. The manager inevitably begins to chase the one of us he considers the ringleader, and as he does this the rest of us sneak in and save one seat for whomever is still being chased. Then one of us rushes to the door from the inside of the movie theatre and calls out for our friend. The manager runs into the theatre, in the dark, while our outside friend sneaks in and hides, as per plan, in some chosen spot until the movie begins.

Of course it is not enough for us to see the entire show for nothing then leave quietly. No. So we construct an equally offensive exit. As we are leaving the theatre we create some commotion near the back of the audience. The manager sees his opportunity and begins to reach out for our necks. But we are now running in a variety of directions. We let him chase us up and down the aisles while one of us positions him self next to one of the two huge exist doors facing the audience from each side of the screen because in late afternoons opening one of these doors fills the theatre with sunlight so no one in the audience can see the screen. By doing this we irritate everyone, for that great scream from an angry audience.

Usually opening the door is Carl's job since he has more strength and the doors must open on time so we can run through them and close them just in time to slam them shut against the manager. This plan once almost backfires. I'm our advance man, meaning I'm the one to irritate the manager, face to face, then insult him, and let him chase me and even let him come close to catching me to tease him. So, this time I play the role perfectly and when he is about to capture me I begin laughing hysterically, virtually unable to run away. But Carl appropriately opens the exit doors, sunlight streams onto an angry audience, and I am about to be caught.

Carl is too good a friend to permit this to happen, so he pushes the door back enough (since they will then swing to close shut on their own), runs up the aisle to grab me by my arm, and drags me out into the sunlight just in time for the door to slam shut against the manager. Carl and I then run all along Myrtle Avenue under the sound of the rusty El train, which creaks as if it's laughing with us as we howl in the joy of being "bad boys."

One Saturday I go to the Peerless movie theatre by myself for the first show in the early evening. I do this because I want to see what adults are seeing. Also, the early show lets out before dark so I can get home early enough, although technically speaking I have no curfew, only common sense that if I'm gone until ten p.m. I might develop a curfew. Seeing this movie changed my life, and now after many years I realize it was the seed of my entire career. More than an answer, this movie revealed all the tools for my future work. The film was *The Search*, Montgomery Clift's first movie.

Sitting among adults in my lucky argyle sweater, I identified with this story of a lost German boy at the end of World War II. I was seeing war the way we should all see it, devastating, like the end of the world, Europe crumpled into heaps of rubble. That was a true eye-opener. Suddenly I understood my mother's refusal to explain war to me and realized her fears while my father was away. This was my most memorable experience of projecting myself into someone's story, something I have been very capable of doing ever since. That boy was alone, scared, wondering whether someone would rescue him as he searched for his mother. My childhood questions were answered with images, music, and feelings that went deep into me. Ever since, whenever I have the opportunity to leap into novels, plays, or poems, I discover answers that are accompanied with real emotions.

❉

NANCY EXPLAINS as I leave her office, "It's next door to Fr. Watson's entrance."

True, I have to go to the bathroom, but mostly I have to be by myself. I'm falling apart. My stomach is churning and feels sickly, as it always does in times of stress. Even at my age, I've experienced enough stress to recognize pang.

❉

ITALIANS SHARE THE STRUGGLES of their family openly. The night before I am to receive confirmation, around four thirty a.m. in the month of May 1950, my parents wake me as Theresa looks on.

"Anthony! Wake up," My father turns on my bed lamp.

"Whaaat!?"

"Wake up"

"What time is it?"

"Four thirty. We just spoke to Aunt Josie."

"What's the matter?"

"Grandpa died."

I am speechless. My mother adds, emotionally.

"He had a heart attack."

My father tells me.

"We're leaving in a little while."

"I'm going with you."

My father insists.

"Grandpa would want you to be confirmed. Later you'll go to the funeral parlor. Uncle Tommy will come here and go with you to your confirmation."

Then he and Theresa leave my room.

I ask my mother, "Does Aunt Anna know?"

"How could she know? We just found out ourselves."

"Is anybody gonna tell her?"

"That's all she would need now that she's getting better."

"When will you tell her?"

"When she gets out of the hospital. Go back to sleep. You have time."

I stop her.

"Why did Grandpa have a heart attack?"

"He watched Aunt Anna suffer her whole life. Then he watched her in that place. How much more could he take?"

Her answer makes her cry. Then she leaves.

That morning I sit during confirmation as the priest delivers his sermon. I am depressed.

"The child is father to the man. Today your souls are filled with grace from the sacrament of Confirmation. Now you become soldiers in the army of Christ to make this a better world."

I angrily speak in a clear voice, "We couldn't make it any worse."

My classmates are shocked that I would say such a thing.

I am being confirmed without my godmother, my grandmother, or my grandfather. Those who love me the most are gone. Later that day, I stand over my grandfather in his coffin and visualize his smiling face when we ate onions, cheese, bread and wine. Then I kiss him, gently.

※

IN THE HEADMASTER'S BATHROOM, I throw up, flush the toilet, and sit on the floor in a cold sweat to pull myself together before returning to Nancy's office.

CHAPTER 4

AUNT ANNA RETURNS HOME. We travel the width of Brooklyn to the Avenue U Apartment for Sunday dinner. Aunt Josie opens the door. We hear voices of our relatives in the dining room. Aunt Dottie is speaking to Aunt Anna.

"Anna, this'll make you more comfortable. Let me put it behind your back."

Aunt Gracie is getting others to sit. "Tommy, sit here."

Aunt Rosie offers her sons to sit in the kitchen.

"Junior and Alfred'll eat in the kitchen."

Aunt Dottie insists, "No, let them stay with us. We set the card table. Come here and sit!"

Aunt Josie whispers to us as she closes the apartment door.

"You're here just in time to eat. She knows about Poppa. Be careful what you say."

I walk slowly, behind the others. I'm afraid. I've waited to see her for so long, prayed for her return at Mass and communion every day, but now that the moment is here I'm afraid to look. Aunt Josie tells us while we walk to the dining room.

"We thought you got caught in traffic."

At the opening into the dining room, I'm shocked the moment I see her. She looks like a frightened boy. She is sitting on two bed pillows with another pillow behind her back. She is very skinny with short, straight black hair. Clearly she has been altered. Her hair is lifeless. Is that what those shock treatments do? I'm angry. She looks frightened, as if she has no idea who we are. Aunt Gracie is speaking to her as if she is mentally challenged.

"Anna, Helen and Vinnie are here. And look, Anthony and Theresa too. Do you see them?"

Theresa goes to kiss her.

"Hi, Aunt Anna."

Theresa is always an equal with each member of the family. Her grace with the aunts and uncles is tremendous because she basically feels she is one of them, not one of the nieces and nephews. My mother kisses Aunt Anna.

"You look wonderful."

And my father does the same.

"It's good to have you back. Congratulations."

"Vinnie, sit here."

"No, Grace, that's your seat."

"Sit, please. I never eat. You know me."

Aunt Josie completes the arrangements.

"Come, Theresa, Helen, sit."

She turns and sees me still standing in the doorjamb.

"What are you doing there? Sit over here."

She leads me.

"Come on, move, Anthony, you're like lead."

I sit staring down at my empty plate.

"Anna," Gracie explains, "Anthony went to Mass and communion every day you were away so you would get better. Even Saturdays! He was like the mailman, rain or shine."

Dottie places chicken soup for me.

"Watch out. It's very hot."

Josie and Rosie bring in more bowls.

In her very loud voice Aunt Rosie asks her husband.

"Tommy you want Parmesan? Tommy?"

"What?! Rosie? I can hear you. Stop screaming. Jesus!"

"Parmesan?"

"Yeah . . . put it in."

She puts a spoonful over his soup.

Aunt Josie sees that I am not eating.

"Anthony, eat. What's the matter with you?"

But I cannot speak, or even look up. Aunt Josie assumes my soup is too hot.

"Blow on it."

Josie and Dottie sit to eat.

Gracie tells me. "I'll eat your soup. It's okay. You'll wait for the lasagna. I know you."

As they eat I secretly glance up. Dottie is feeding Aunt Anna. No one knows what to say.

There is painful silence.

Finally, Aunt Rosie, unaware that there has been silence, since her world is always silent, inadvertently breaks the ice.

"Anna, you want escarole in your soup?"

Aunt Anna shakes her head "No."

More silence.

Then Rosie adds, again without having noticed the silence.

"Anna? Remember the escarole in olive oil I brought you in the nuthouse?"

The family freezes as if its joint spine stiffened.

"How could I forget? You brought it every week."

And she speaks in the voice that was always Aunt Anna. The tension at the table dissolves into laughter.

"You said you liked it, that's why I brought it."

"Sure, I loved it. But the other patients used to make fun of you. Anna, the one with the escarole, you know, the deaf one? She belongs in here, not us. How come they let her out?'"

"I'd be better off. Twelve years with Tommy is worse than the nuthouse."

Tommy wants to know.

"Who's in the nuthouse?"

Aunt Anna is her old self.

"Remember the old lady across from me who always hugged her dolls?"

Aunt Josie says. "Sure, the one who ate your chocolates and never said thank you."

"She decided to marry Willie when he visits next time. Good thing I'm out of there. She was serious. Said he was better looking than her four husbands, and that she had a nice big bed at home waiting for him."

Aunt Josie proclaims, "Anything would be better than that *puttana* he married."

Gracie warns, "Josie, the kids!"

But Josie is having fun.

"Junior, you know what *puttana* means?"

Junior says. "No, what?"

"A good for nothing bum. Someone who sits on her ass all day."

Junior and Alfred, my two cousins, chant, *"puttana!"*

My mother steps in.

"Okay, wise guys, that's enough."

Aunt Rosie tells Uncle Tommy, "Tommy, *'puttana,'* listen to them."

Uncle Tommy is always five beats behind every conversation.

"Who's the *puttana?*"

His sons, Junior and Alfred, continue.

"puttana! puttana!"

Gracie accuses Josie.

"See what you started?"

"Good. Now they'll know what to avoid when they get married."

Junior announces.

"I'm gonna marry a *puttana!*"

The family welcomes these opportunities to laugh. Aunt Josie is relentless.

"You better learn to cook. Or you and your *puttana* will starve to death."

Dottie collects the empty bowls and says.

"Gracie, bring in the lasagna. Theresa, get the salad and put the roasted chickens on the platters."

The family disperses to gather the rest of dinner. As Aunt Rosie exits she proclaims loudly, "She'll be her old self in no time. Fatten her up a bit, that's all."

I cross to sit next to Anna. The family continues to speak loudly. Aunt Josie tells others as they go into kitchen, "She remembered the food."

Gracie responds.

"Isn't that something?"

My mother adds.

"We knew it would work."

Aunt Rosie triumphs, at high volume.

"And you all told me not to bring the escarole."

Alone now, I ask my godmother.

"Was it hard . . . in the hospital, I mean?"

"It was awful. Stay strong, Anthony! Don't ever let your nerves get the best of you. When you lose who you are, you lose everything. Our health is all we have."

"But you recovered."

"I'm lucky."

"What are the shock treatments like?"

"Frightening. I don't wish them on anyone."

"Do you mind my asking?"

"No. You should know."

"Will it ever happen again?"

"Not if I can help it."

The family re-enters with a feast. Aunt Anna jokes.

"God forbid this family should miss a meal."

My mother carries in a platter with chicken and mushrooms.

"Only six years! Those pigs left a mess."

This disturbs Theresa.

"We're moving?"

My mother explains why we're returning to the apartment we vacated during the war.

"We can be near the family again."

Aunt Josie wonders.

"How did you hear about it?"

"I asked Mr. Pernetti to let me know when an apartment was vacant. Whoever thought it would be the same one?"

Theresa gets right to the point. "Where we gonna sleep?"

"You and Anthony in one bedroom and Daddy and me in the other. Like before."

"That was before the war. I'm not sleeping in the same room with him."

"Well you have no choice. We can't live in the projects any longer."

"Why not?"

"It's no place for a teenage daughter. Can't you figure that out?"

"I can take care of myself and I want my own bedroom."

"When you get married, you'll get one."

My mother always had that special punch. Theresa storms out of the dining room. Gracie calls after her.

"Theresa, come on now, come back."

My mother continues.

"Anthony starts taking entrance exams all over the city for high school. The projects served its purpose. Now we must get away from there."

Josie says as they bring in coffee.

"Dottie thinks Anna should sell her cookies to the bakery."

"Will you?" I ask.

But Aunt Anna is too clever for any of us.

"Anthony, have you ever seen our family sell anything? Aunt Gracie would be sneaking cookies to the church or to whomever else she feels needs cookies for nothing. We'll all get into heaven just because of her. She's been buying us passes for years."

Aunt Gracie says, "Anthony. Aunt Josie, Anna, Dottie, and I are moving into a house in two weeks. You'll help your godmother with the garden."

"Do you know anything about it?" I ask Aunt Anna.

"You and me, Anthony, we'll figure it out. How hard can it be?

CHAPTER 5

I AM SOAKING WET ON THE FLOOR of the headmaster's bathroom. I sit back against the door and use my handkerchief to dry my sweat. I also feel feverish, but I know I have to cover it up or someone will send me home. I leave the bathroom when the three p.m. school bell rings, as preppies leave for the day.

I enter Nancy's office.

"Is he back?"

"Not yet. You all right?"

"I have a headache, that's all."

I cover the front of myself with my zippered jacket. I sit. I'm shaking. The door opens and a fifty-year-old lay teacher, dressed in a suit and tie under a flowing black professorial robe, hands Nancy a list of names.

"Mr. Nebot, what can I do for you?"

"Nothing, thank you. Father here?"

"No."

"Tell him I'll talk to him tomorrow about the new logo for the Stag."

He leaves.

"What's the Stag, I ask?"

"Our school newspaper. You sure you're okay?"

I nod.

"You look a bit pale. Maybe you should come back tomorrow."

"I couldn't sleep last night."

"Why not go home, get a good night's rest and come back?"

"No, I'm fine."

"I'm positive one of us could help."

"I'm fine. Really."

She knows not to intrude.

I wait.

※

THE DAY I HAD TAKEN the entrance exam, I return home feeling like I'm on fire, knowing I have found the place to go to school. Flushing through my soul is an expansion of my universe. Many thoughts I never ever had would now become a way of life because the very environment of a school dedicated to thought and literature could open the world to me. I knew this deep inside myself. I had stepped in front of an epiphany, and I was elated.

I am trying to communicate this excitement to the family for a half hour. They seem uninterested. My mother is stretching lace curtains onto a wooden frame with dozens of little pins around the edges. My father and Theresa are watching the World Series. My father repeats the same question.

"Brooklyn Tech?"

"No. Prep. Brooklyn Prep."

"Never heard of it."

Mom says, "I heard Brooklyn Tech's a good school."

"This is Brooklyn Prep. It's run by Jesuits Sr. Elizabeth called them. I really like it there."

"If you get into Brooklyn Tech, you should go there. My Aunt Mamie's son became an Accountant. Makes terrific money, which is good now they have three children."

This strains my nerves.

"Who wants to be an accountant?"

Theresa puts the evil eye on me.

"You haven't even passed the test yet."

"I will. I passed all the others."

"Don't be so sure."

My mother continues as she goes to prepare dinner.

'Don't count your chickens before they hatch."

Theresa hates my confidence.

"Your head gets bigger by the minute."

I resort.

"Yeah, well, you'll see."

My father offers snow in the winter.

"Well, if you get in, we'll think about it."

"There's nothing to think about. I'm going no matter what any of you say."

Calling from kitchen, my mother changes the topic.

"Theresa, mash the potatoes. The steaks will be ready in a few minutes."

Theresa leaves for the kitchen and says.

"Make sure mine's cooked all the way."

I am exasperated.

"Doesn't anybody care?"

Taking steaks from the broiler my mother reveals her attitude.

"One school is as good as another if you really want to learn."

"This is different. It's special."

I try in vain to convince her.

"You should see it. Sr. Elizabeth says the Jesuits are the best teachers, they're men of the world".

This upset my mother.

"Enough already. You're giving me a headache. You want to be a man of the world, get a job."

"And that the Jesuits fight for what they believe in."

Theresa rails, "Then you don't have to go there. You fight for everything already."

"I'm going to school there!"

Food usually helps my mother win.

"Dinner's ready."

The three of them sit down to eat. The game is still on television in the living room. And I'm left standing over them hoping to get their support.

Theresa moves to the stove to fry her steak.

"This steak is bloody."

Mom tells me.

"Anthony, don't let your steak get cold. It's rare, the way you like it."

I demand to know.

"What are you all afraid of?"

This gets their attention. My mother responds.

"What the hell are you talking about?"

I hit the mark. They are afraid, but of what? It has taken me many, many years, but by now I think I might have come close to understanding such fears. My mother feared she would lose me, possibly to the priesthood, which at the time would have been a correct fear. Also, she would no longer have me there, and my mother and I were virtually the same person, so she didn't want the separation. My mother had certain psychic feelings, so basically she knew at fourteen I would be gone for good if I found that alternate world. With her commitment to family, that would be inadequate. But my mother's greatness was her motherhood, so for my happiness she would willingly suffer the consequence.

Theresa feared I might prove not to be the sissy she christened me from birth. But it wasn't a lack of love or a mean-mindedness, which on the surface it seemed to be. No, it was her subconscious need for me to find the technique necessary to rescue her from her angers. But since Theresa never revealed her vulnerability, who knew she had any need? The only fear my father could have had was that I might reach too high towards heaven, and keeping me earthbound was important to him. Fortunately, I was enough of a brat not to care, so I set my sail upon Brooklyn Prep.

※

NOW, WITH THE NEW HOUSE my aunts purchased, old though it is, I am learning a great deal from Aunt Anna about flowers, mulch, and fertilizing. Also, the house is only a mile away from our apartment on Coney Island Avenue, so going back and forth to help Aunt Anna is easy and our conversations are always worth the walk. And, as we dig, we discuss just about anything.

"Most people live dumb lives. The people in the projects are really sad."

"That'll never be you, Anthony."

"But I want to help people like that and I don't know how. I ask questions and never get the answers. I want to know things. I'm always told to keep my nose clean. What's our family afraid of?"

"People. The world. Ourselves."

"Why?"

"We never feel we can have things other people have. We are grateful just to be alive, which is a good thing, but afraid to ask for more. We never want to do anything wrong."

"But why, Aunt Anna? No one in our family does anything wrong."

"Around the time we were born, they kept killing Italians all over America whether you did anything wrong or not. There was a lynching of eleven Italians in New Orleans and executions of Sacco and Vanzetti in Massachusetts. Innocent, working people! So we grew up frightened. Our fears made us weak. We are afraid to go into the world, and every time we have to face some serious problem, we fall apart. You've seen that for yourself."

"How do I become strong?"

"Fight for things that are important."

"Isn't school worth fighting for?"

"If this is the right place, make them understand. They want the best for you."

"I don't think they do."

"Your parents will do anything to help you. Make them see that what you want is a good thing. Only a few of us ever went to high school and we never paid for it."

"How do I make them understand? I won't really know until I go there."

"If you can't figure it out, who will? How can you get strong if someone else does it for you? There are many times in life when it is only up to you, no one else. Solve this problem, Anthony, you'll be on your way."

※

NANCY MOVES AROUND her office quietly. Though I am asleep I am somewhat able to sense what is happening. I am basically in a daze of exhaustion, tension and nerves.

※

MY ACCEPTANCE LETTER to my parents arrives in early November of 1952. I wait for my mother to return from work, follow her into and out of the grocery store, arguing with her.

"So you got in? We can't afford it anyway."

"But I have to go there."

"Read those prices for tuition, books, travel. It's too expensive."

"But there's nowhere else."

"Are you stupid or something? Nowhere else! You live in New York with dozens of high schools. You've been accepted everywhere."

"Not like this one."

"We never planned to pay for high school."

We arrive at the stoop of our building.

"Why did you let me take all those tests?"

"We didn't let you. You went yourself. You want freedom to do whatever you want, and then I have to pay for it?"

"But this is the one. I have to register immediately. I've been accepted in the first group. Three thousand kids took the test. They only accept three hundred."

"Pick one of the other schools."

"I don't want any of the others."

"Well you have to, and that's that. It's not your choice."

"But most of them cost some money. What's the difference?"

"And you picked the most expensive one on the other side of Brooklyn. You want to travel several hours a day just to go to high school? Go to Madison in the neighborhood. It doesn't cost anything and you can walk to it."

"I liked the Jesuits."

"You've had enough church already. Finish your education. Get a good job. Start a family. You'll have a good life. These priests will only fill your head with nonsense. It's not your job to save the world. Stick your neck out someone will chop your head off."

She enters our building. I shout after her.

"I'm going to Brooklyn Prep whether you like it or not."

"Over my dead body."

"If that's what it takes!"

I know how to hurt her. I see her entire body cringe.

❇

AROUND CHRISTMAS EVE I am pacing near our lit Christmas tree as my mother, father, and Theresa watch I Love Lucy and eat ice cream.

"You have to find the money."

"You always have to be different. That's all this is about. We can't afford it."

My mother repeats that too many times.

"Stop saying that."

"Well go to Brooklyn Prep without money and see how far that gets you."

She is impossible.

"I can't understand why you won't do this."

My father shows some interest.

"What would you learn there that you can't learn anywhere else?"

"I don't know. I've never been there."

But mom argues, "You always put yourself first. The money it would cost us means there are things we would do without. Is that fair?"

I'm fighting for my life.

"So do without!"

This thrills Theresa.

"Bingo! He's your son. Come up and choose your prize."

My mother tries to reason.

"With both of us working, we're barely recovering from the war. Now you want us to go into debt again?"

"By the time you recover, I'll be finished with high school. This is my chance. I won't get another one."

Theresa triumphs. "Give it up Anthony, you're not gonna win."

She gets up to wash her dish and pushes me backwards in passing. As the TV audience laughs uproariously, I make the strongest fist I can and punch her in the stomach. Theresa rises in the air, then flops to the floor on her ass. My father jumps up from his chair.

"Are you crazy? You never hit a woman in the stomach. Don't you understand?"

"I understand."

I understand in that moment that it is up to me to defend myself and up to me to win this battle. I also understand that Theresa will never punch me again. My father helps Theresa up as he speaks to me.

"You've made yourself unhappy by pursuing something we told you not to pursue."

My mother agrees with him.

"Your head is too big for our pocketbook."

"You always told me my education was the most important thing in the world."

My father agrees.

"It is."

"Well I found the place to have that education and you won't let me."

"Why are you so sure?"

"I knew it the day I took the test."

"Do you have friends there?"

"No."

"Are your friends planning to go there?"

"No."

"Had you ever heard of this school before you went for the test?"

"No."

"Then how do you know?"

"What's the difference? I know. That's all. I'm positive. You told me to pick the thing in life that comes easiest to me, and that I like the best. You said if I did that I would be successful."

"What a memory you have."

"So I picked it."

"I was talking about a job."

"How can I find the best job if I don't have the best education? I don't know what I want to do with my life yet. Isn't that what an education is for?"

"Don't make yourself so miserable."

"I passed in the top percentage throughout the entire city."

"You should be very proud of that."

"This is my last chance, Dad. They're accepting the third group of applicants, and because I'm in the first group I can still register. If I don't register tomorrow, I can never go there. Classes start in a month."

Theresa turns on the loud vacuum to end all discussion.

❄

WHEN I WAKE UP, Nancy is straightening up her desk. I see darkness outside the window. This upsets me.

"He didn't come back?"
"No, and I have to get to night classes."
"Can I wait in the hallway?"
"The school will not allow you to just stand in the hallway."
"Can I wait for him outside?"
"How would you know who he is?"
"I'll ask."
"Let's wait a little longer."
She has typed letters.
"I need him to sign these letters."
I wait.

※

IT IS TEN P.M. on Jan 24, 1953. All signs of Christmas are cleared away. I'm on the floor watching the roller derby. Theresa is watching from the sofa. My parents are standing over me. My father says to me.

"You have no choice. You waited too long to register at other schools."

Theresa turns the television up and changes her seat so they won't block her view.

"Most boys would love to go to Tech."
"I wanted to go to Brooklyn Prep."

My mother hammers nails in my coffin.

"It's too late."
"I hate you."
"The hell with you then!"

She heads to the kitchen and continues.

"Leave him alone. He'll go to Tech tomorrow. He has no other choice."

My father kneels next to me.

"Look, you haven't even tried it. You're really gonna like it. I promise you."

"I hated it when I took the test. I told you that."
"You passed. They invited you. Tomorrow you start."
"Prep starts tomorrow too."
"Yes, but it is too late now. Remember?"

"I remember. And I'll never forget what you have done to me."
"They won't accept you now."
"You should all go to hell."
My mother tries to coerce me.
"I'll tell you what. Go to Tech for one year. Then go to Prep."
"They won't let me in then and you know it. You think I'm an idiot?"
"Well, it's too late in any case. Why don't you register tomorrow at one of the other schools if you hate Tech so much."
"Because I hated them all."
"How can there be only one school? You're so stupid you need a special school?"

※

SO ON JANUARY 25, the day of my fourteenth birthday, I sit in homeroom of Brooklyn Tech. I have been through each class throughout the day, and I sit next to the open door and listen to noisy corridors. In dry, flat, and irritable vocal tones Mr. Hutchins, my homeroom teacher, fills us in.

"You come to this room twice a day, nine a.m. and 2:50 p.m., unless you are also taking mechanical drawing and accounting. This is homeroom. You are assigned to me until June. Any special problems you may have with other classes or teachers should come through me. If I can't help, I'll send you to someone else."

I sit stone-faced with my stack of textbooks: Economics. Algebra. Calculus I. Mechanical Drawing. Biology. Accounting. English. History.

"Any questions?"
Silence.
"Then, until tomorrow this class is over."

※

JUST AFTER FIVE O'CLOCK, the light in Fr. Watson's office goes on. Nancy is excited.

"He's back."

She grabs the letters and enters Watson's office, closing the glass-paneled door behind her. My stomach begins to churn again. I feel I am about to learn what losing is all about.

BROOKLYN ODYSSEY 119

※

LAST NIGHT I RETURNED HOME from Brooklyn Tech to the family's attempt to celebrate my birthday. But I will have none of it. My mother makes my favorites, but I am not about to let her cooking win this day. She, Theresa, and my father eat breaded pork chops, eggplant parmigiana, spinach sautéed with olive oil and garlic, mashed potatoes, and carrots. A homemade lemon meringue pie is cooling on the kitchen windowsill. I sit and stare at my favorite foods as if they are poison this night.

My father says, "How was school today? And, by the way, Happy Birthday."

I mash down a lump in potatoes, to make a point. My father tries again to engage me.

"I asked you a question."

On my way home I vowed never to speak to any of them again.

"Look Anthony, we're getting fed up with you. I asked you how was school today?"

"Fine."

"That's it? Just fine?"

"That's it."

"What courses are you studying?"

"It doesn't matter."

"Why doesn't it matter?"

"It doesn't, that's all."

"Look, you better make the best of your high school years."

My mother is firm.

"Let him find out for himself. If he fails then he'll learn the hard way."

But my father tries.

"What classes will you be studying?"

"It doesn't matter."

"Why doesn't it matter?"

I explode.

"Because I'm never going back! You can prevent me from going to the school I want because you won't give me the money. But you can't force me to go to a school I don't want. You're all liars. I need to find out what I want to do with my life. Not what you want me to do."

My mother fights back.

"Brooklyn Tech is an excellent school."

"I don't want to be an accountant, or an engineer, or a biologist. Can't you get that into your heads? You want me to waste my life doing what I don't want to do. But I'm never going back."

She asks.

"What does that mean?"

"I won't go tomorrow or any other day, and you might as well know it."

My father wonders.

"What will you do?"

"I'll go to libraries and museums. I'll teach myself, but I won't go back to Tech."

I try to eat to recover some dignity. My father is trying to understand me.

"How can you be so sure of what you want?"

Then I fall apart completely. I begin spitting potatoes through excruciating tears.

"You always told me to do with my life whatever I thought was best for me. And I'm trying to do that."

I run into the living room. I cannot stop crying. My father follows me.

"Calm down . . . come on, relax . . . Hey!"

He shakes me, but I can't stop the floodgates.

"How can anything be this important?"

From the kitchen my mother calls.

"Come back to eat. He'll go to school or he won't. He's spoiled rotten. We always gave in. This time, Anthony, you're not gonna win, you hear?"

"I can't learn what I need at Tech."

She enters the living room.

"So go to Madison. What do you think all the other kids in the neighborhood do?"

"When you go to work tomorrow, I'm staying home. I'm not wasting four years of my life."

"Since you're staying home tomorrow, take the wash to the Laundromat. You can be my helper. I'm happy to hear it."

"Don't you want me to have the right education?"

"Your head is full of nonsense. Of course, I want you to have the right education. But you always have big ideas. What do you want to do this time, solve the problems of the world? Jesuits, men of the world, fighters; what is this war you're preparing for? The war ended seven years ago. Become a teacher. You'll have a good life. I'm scared to death you're gonna become a priest."

"I want to be a psychiatrist."

"A psychiatrist? What happened to pianist, dancer? Your head is too busy. I've heard nothing but 'I want' from you all your life. And always things you can't have."

"I can't have them because you won't let me. But I'm not wasting any more time listening to any of you. You're not interested in me."

"Are you nuts?"

"You're interested in my becoming like you. But I want my own life."

My father warns.

"We're your family, Anthony, never forget that."

I reply as sarcastically as I can.

"Believe me, I never will."

My father enters a dark question, "Can this school be so important that you would fight your own family?"

"Yes."

"I can't understand that."

"When I went to Prep, I felt different, like I could find what I wanted. Now it's too late."

My father offers.

"Okay, okay calm down. I'll make a deal."

My mother insists.

"We agreed not to give in,"

"This is different."

"No deals," she insists.

"Go inside and let me take care of this."

But she was not stoppable.

"Prep is all the way across Brooklyn. What's he gonna spend all day long traveling? What kind of education is that? Go to Madison or Tech. In the fall change to St. Augustine's if you want. It's a diocesan school, two stops away"

"I hated St. Augustine's."

She heads back to the kitchen.

"Of course you hated it. I would have been surprised if you liked it. My whole stomach's turning sour."

My father takes over.

"Listen to me. You go to Prep tomorrow, and if they let you in, your mother and I will find the money."

She yells from the kitchen.

"That's ridiculous."

"First they have to let him in. We'll find the money, if they let him in."

She realizes it could never happen so she shuts up.

"Do you hear me? If they let you in."

"You know it's too late now and they won't let me in."

"To be honest with you, you're right. I don't think they will let you in. But if they do, we'll pay for it. You will have won. We don't want to lose our son, especially to hate. You're our family. We're not used to anyone wanting the things you want. Maybe this is the right school. We just don't know anything about it. If you get in tomorrow that's where you will go. And we will make the most of it. Deal?"

"Deal."

"If you get in, you will have deserved it. But if you don't get in, you go to Brooklyn Tech the next day. Or Madison. And you make the best of that. No more scenes."

Mom chimes in.

"We always give in."

Dad finishes.

"No more scenes after tomorrow!"

We return to the kitchen as Theresa brings the lemon meringue pie to the table. She holds it out to me and sings in her meanest and most sarcastic tone.

"Happy Birthday to you!"

No one else joins in her unfriendly rendition.

"Happy birthday, brother, happy birthday, spoiled brat!"

Theresa places the pie on the table, takes the flat side of the knife and smashes the pie into four pieces.

※

I CAN HEAR NANCY and Fr. Watson talking softly, but I cannot make out what they're saying. I try to adjust my shirt in my pants and straighten out the sweater Aunt Anna knitted for me years ago that finally fits, but my hands are too nervous.

I stand, waiting.

Fr. Watson comes to the door with Nancy at his side. "You want to see me?"

"Yes."

"Come in."

We pass Nancy, who closes the door behind us. His office is large, simple but well furnished. Fr. Watson is a modestly built man with thin gold-framed eyeglasses, about fifty-five years old. He is the perfect image of a bank president with penetrating eyes, a no nonsense guy. "I understand you have been waiting since nine o'clock."

"Yes."

"Well, what can I do for you?"

"I want to go to school here."

"So that's the mystery."

He stares through me in a way that makes me feel he is trying to find something he doesn't like about me, to help him deny my dream of entering his school. So he listens after each of my answers to evaluate who and what I am, to make his decision.

"May I ask why you would speak to no one else?"

"Things sometimes get confused. I didn't want anything to go wrong."

Fr. Watson takes this in, almost as if he is understanding something that makes no sense.

"If I came back later tonight?"

"I would have waited."

Again, Watson sizes up my answer.

"You mean this semester?"

"Yes."

"Did you take the entrance exam?"

"Last year."

"Well that's good. What grammar school?"

"St. Brendan's. East 14th Street, Avenue O."

"Then your folder will be here."

He begins to turn towards his file cabinets, but stops instead to ask me, "Do you realize that we began classes yesterday?"

"Yes."

"We closed the registration a while ago. We filled up all the seats."

I wait for more but offer him no way out.

"Did you ever receive an invitation to register?"

"Yes. My parents received this letter that I was accepted in the first group." (Anthony hands the letter to Fr. Watson)

"And why didn't you?"

"My family felt I could go to any one of the other schools near home rather than travel every day."

"And now?"

"They've changed their mind."

I fear what is coming and assume it is written all over my face. I suspect Fr. Watson needs some excuse to say no and may find something wrong in my folder. Watson turns away and leaves me standing in the middle of his office. He quickly checks the letter, then he rummages through a file cabinet and finds my folder. There are times in life when your heart stops, or so it seems. Perhaps it took him only half a second, but whatever time it took while I stood aimless in the middle of his office was my lifetime. He opens my folder but before he reads he speaks to me, as if he too needs a bottom line and he feels he might have one.

"Why do you want to go to school here?"

I waited all day but never prepared for his question. I fear my inability to have an answer will be the cause of his refusal. It never dawned on me I would need an answer. After all, I was here, waiting all day. I hoped that would be positive enough. By having no answer I was demonstrating that I was not ready to go to this school. In any case I didn't have one.

"I don't know."

"Well, what made you feel you want to go to school here?"

I tried to find something intelligent to say but I could not think of anything important.

"The day I took the test, I heard . . ."

Suddenly I could not think at all. I became frozen.

"Heard what?"

I could only tell him a simple truth, even if it meant losing everything.

"Talk."

"'Talk?'"

I had nothing in my stomach to throw up or I would have. Everything inside was churning.

"What do you mean talk?"

"The teachers made sense. I liked them. I want to learn from them."

"You were aware of this while you took the test?"

"Yes they made the test easier because they were funny. They made us laugh."

"How interesting."

Watson stares at me for a long beat. Now he seems to be trying to find the right answer. Then he opens my folder. He reads through several pages carefully, turns to investigate me and compare whatever he is finding in my papers. Then he returns to read other pages.

I wait.

Finally he looks to me.

"You can go to school here. You have the grades and obviously the spunk. We'll be lucky to have you."

I am speechless. He and I stare at each other for what I can only recall as interminable while I fear there will be some surprise objection, some avoidance, like "But we will have to wait until next year." He keeps staring to interpret me. I provide nothing to help him. He closes my folder. When he turns to close the drawer of the file cabinet, I press my finger against the side of my cheek to prevent myself from crying. My stomach is hurting. My head is hot. My feet are cold. And my shorts are moist. Then I feign an itch on my nose in case he turns and catches me. I wait in anticipation for the final outcome of his decision. Father Watson turns to me.

"You begin tomorrow at nine a.m. Will you be ready?"

I suppress tears, fears, and joys to answer.

"I'll be ready."

"Come to my office at 8:40 and I'll give you your schedule. I want to be sure everything works out the first day."

"I'll be here. 8:40."

"See you then."

Fr. Watson opens his door and I leave his office. I go into Nancy's office to get my jacket and tell her.

"I'm going to school here. Tomorrow."

"How did you do that?"

"I don't know."

Fr. Watson comes to his open door.

"What do you like to be called?"

I'm batting a thousand now.

"Tony!"

"Okay, Tony. See you tomorrow."

I leave the office and run through the dimly lit corridor, my face flush in ecstatic happiness. It is dark outside. I know there is nothing ever again I cannot do, so I leap high off the steps to kick bells. But instead of landing on my feet, I crash into two metal garbage cans at the foot of the stairs, waking the neighborhood.

An old Yiddish lady with groceries rushes to help me.

"Oy vey es mere! Zindala."

She mutters to herself as she tries to get me to my feet.

"Vus il ich tun? Du hust schmertzen?"

I rise and assure her.

"I just have to practice."

Then I run, and run, and run to the train, crying with joy all though the ride home. At Kings Highway station, I leap down the stairs to the street, then run and run and run again until I get to the stoop at 1877 Coney Island Avenue. As I am about to enter our building I turn back to the street and try bells, but fall down the stone stairs. I come up this time with a bloody nose. I run upstairs into the apartment, exploding with joy.

My mother is on the phone but is the first to see me.

BROOKLYN ODYSSEY 127

"Oh my God, they beat you up."

"I got in."

My father asks from behind his newspaper.

"They let you in?"

My mother is nervous.

"We waited all day. Are you okay? Why did they beat you up?

"I got in."

My father asks, stunned.

"Did they not want to talk to us?"

"No. I got in."

He asks.

"How did you do that?"

"I don't know."

My mother hands me a wet towel.

"Wipe that blood from your face."

My mother gets the food from the stove.

"I start in the morning."

My father is so honest.

"What an accomplishment. You must be very proud of yourself."

I sit down. Theresa and my father stand across from me. My mother pours soup into my dish.

Theresa sits opposite me.

"You did good, brother."

With my voice breaking, barely able to talk,

"I got in."

ABOUT THE AUTHOR

Tony Giordano wrote his musical, *Habana Carnaval* in Cuba, 2004, then returned to direct it, 2006. With Neil Proto he co-adapted a Dutch musical by composer Dirk Brosse, about Sacco & Vanzetti, now called *The American Dream,* which Tony directed in a concert version at the Shubert Theatre in New Haven. He also wrote three books under a subtitle, called the art of men acting: *Brooklyn Odyssey, Tonight I Won't Be Acting,* and *Not For Prophet.*

Tony directed New York productions of *Ladyhouse Blues* with Jo Henderson, *G.R. Point* with John Heard, *Snow Orchid* with Olympia Dukakis and Peter Boyle, *The Chekhov Sketchbook* with Joseph Buloff, Bill Gibson's *Handy Dandy* with James Whitmore and Audra Lindley, *Kingdoms* with Armand Assante, and *Mixed Emotions* with Katherine Helmond and Harold Gould. His production of *The Tavern* won Best Director and Best Production from L.A.'s Outer Critics Circle & Dramalogue Awards; and his *Substance of Fire* Best Production from the Florida critics. His *Lend Me A Tenor* was reviewed as "The best production in the history of Trinity Rep." He directed *Asher's Command,* a new play about Israel and Palestine, which won the Kennedy Center's award for new plays. Highlighted among his 150 productions are *Long Day's Journey Into Night* at Canada's Citadel; Yale Rep's *Curse of the Starving Class*, Athol Fugard's *Hello and Goodbye*, and *The Day of the Picnic* starring James Earle Jones; a tour of Miller's *View From the Bridge*; Feydeau's *Hotel Paradiso, Noises Off,* and *Glengarry Glen Ross* at Trinity Rep; Pinter's *The Birthday Party* at the Dallas Theatre Center; and the musicals *She Loves Me, Man of La Mancha, Funny Girl, Funny thing Happened on the Way to the Forum, The Boy Friend,* and *Tomfoolery.*

He received Italy's GRAND CROSS, a lifetime achievement award for his social consciousness to America, and Catholic University's GILBERT for career achievement.

Tony developed original plays at the O'Neill Playwright's Conference for eleven years; directed hour-long dramas for National Public Radio; and both NBC and ABC'S "Another World," "The Doctors," "One Life to Live," and "Loving." He taught directing for the Yale School of Drama. He was the Chairman of the Board and founding member of NY's subsidized Manhattan Plaza and Executive Vice-President of the Society of Stage Directors & Choreographers until he resigned both memberships in protest against corruptions.

Favorite stars he directed are Audra Lindley, James Whitmore, Colleen Dewhurst, Chita Rivera, Dana Andrews. Kay Medford, James Earle Jones, Mary Alice, Katherine Kelmond, Armand Assante, Meryll Streep, John Heard, Joseph Buloff, Fyvush Finkel, and Reizl Boyzak.

Tony was born and raised in Brooklyn, studied with Jesuits at Brooklyn Prep and Fairfield University. He received his MA in Drama from Catholic University.